ALSO BY STEVE CHANDLER

100 Ways to Motivate Yourself

Reinventing Yourself

17 LIES THAT ARE HOLDING YOU BACK
& THE TRUTH THAT WILL SET YOU FREE

17 LIES THAT ARE HOLDING YOU BACK & THE TRUTH THAT WILL SET YOU FREE

STEVE CHANDLER

St. Martin's Griffin ● New York

For Kathy

www.stmartins.com

ISBN 1-58063-215-7   ISBN 978-1-58063-215-7

P1

ACKNOWLEDGMENTS

Steve Hardison for coaching beyond expectations. Fred Knipe for setting the standard. Kathryn Eimers for the grace and style. Lyndon Duke for the power of language. Lindsay Brady for the hypnotherapy. Bill Eimers for the transcendental idea. Jim Brannigan for the representation. Nathaniel Branden for the psychology. Colin Wilson for the philosophy. Deepak Chopra for the dharma. Jess, Steph, Bob, and Marge for the inspiration. Arthur Morey for the editorial counsel. Darlene Brady for the business sense. Terry Hill for the postcards from France. Cindy Chandler for the spirituality. David Chandler for San Diego and Thanksgiving. Danna Fisher for a lifetime of kindness. Scott Richardson for the support. Merlin F. Ludiker for advice from hell.

And to the memory of Tom Moehl, gentle friend, artful spirit.

CONTENTS

1
LYING TO THE SOUL

2
FINDING YOUR DEEPEST POWER

Death is not the most profound loss or tragedy in life. That which dies inside of us as we live is a far greater loss. The loss of possibility, a loss that comes from running our personal rackets, has ravaged the lives of too many individuals who could have otherwise transformed the world.

—Tracy Goss,
The Last Word on Power

The river Jordan

is chilly and cold.

It chills the body,

but not the soul.

—American Folk Song

LIVING IN A
RIVER OF FEAR

This is a book about lies. Not the everyday white lies we use to spare someone's feelings (usually our own). Nor is it about huge public lies like, "I would never do anything to harm Nicole."

These are lies that do more damage than those do.

These are lies to the soul.

These are lies we send down inside ourselves that convince us that we don't have any power.

This is a book dedicated to uncovering a racket—the racket of conning ourselves into believing that deep inside we are helpless. The racket that talks us into believing in our defects instead of our energy.

This con job can become a life-long stratagem of self-deceit. If the lies are not exposed and brought out into the open, they can make fearful infants of us all.

We will see how we chill ourselves down with these lies. How we use them to dampen the fire of the human spirit. And how we think "If I underachieve, so what? At least that's predictable and easy to manage." Operating on a small percentage of our potential may lead to a life of mild misery, but it's misery that's easy to manage, just as a car going at a slow speed is easier to manage than one going 120 miles per hour. Going 120 miles per hour is frightening. And thrilling.

The widespread popularity of self-deceiving might be due to its effectiveness. It gets the job done. It takes us out of the game. It sits us down at the end of the bench so we don't have to play. It even puts a cool towel around our necks, a towel in which we can hide our faces if we become ashamed that the world is passing us by.

We speak these lies of how defeated we are so that they roll down like chilly water onto our souls, down like the river Jordan onto the flame of the spirit. All our lives our lies roll on. Roll on, like the Fugs used to sing, about the mighty river they called the "river of shit."

It was a song about lies.

Every lie we tell ourselves is based on fear. Fear of the unknown. Fear of the fresh and the beautiful. Fear of that daring plunge into unknown beauty. Fear of uncertainty. Fear of being courageous, evolving, and creative. Fear of risking being a total fool. Fear of taking a stand for greatness.

Those fears inspire the lies. The lies give us an easier, softer way to go every time. They remove us from daring action and huge commitments. From inventing a future in the face of total uncertainty.

But the truth is that we don't have to accept anything cold rolling down inside us. We don't have to experience a river of fear. The truth is that we are powerful. We can fight back. We can take our lives into our own hands.

PEOPLE LIE ABOUT THEIR LIMITS

Power grows in us the moment a future dream transforms into present-day action. That's when magic beyond comprehension expands inside the human energy system. That's what happened when Roger Bannnister became the first human to run the four-minute mile. It had become more than just a goal to him. So his mind expanded to let the new power in.

Prior to Bannister, the running world had feared that the human body simply wasn't constructed to run the mile in faster than four minutes. It was feared that the human body would break down at that speed, that bad things would happen. But since that time, many more people have re-routed the river of fear inside them and accomplished even bigger things.

This is true even in the narrow category of the footrace! There are many people over sixty years old who are now bettering earlier Olympic gold medal times (set by runners in their twenties) for the mile. This is because humans are learning to expand their minds while the body merely follows. And while many will say that these faster running times are just because of better vitamins, training, and nutrition, that doesn't really explain it. Because the same improvement hasn't happened with racehorses. Over the same period of time, horses have also had better training and nutrition. They've even had controlled breeding. Yet no such astounding improvements in the times of racehorses has occurred.

Human athletic accomplishments keep soaring beyond what we once believed possible. Human scientific accomplishments keep soaring as well. Human technological accomplishments are keeping pace.

Perhaps the reason is simple: Human beings are finding greater and greater power within their minds. Humans are learning to stop lying about their limits. In this case, a sense of purpose replaces the lies inside the personal motivational system.

We can replace a river of lies with a river of dreams. It's the same imagination that creates both, so why not take the dreams?

These are the seventeen lies that are in the way of those dreams.

And to see them is to see them disappear.

This earth is the distant star we must find a way to reach.

—Nathaniel Branden

1

LYING TO
THE SOUL

Whatever we learn to do, we learn by actually doing it. People come to be builders, for instance, by building, and harp players by playing the harp. In the same way, by doing just acts we come to be just. By doing self-controlled acts, we come to be self-controlled, and by doing brave acts we become brave.

—Aristotle,
Nicomachaen Ethics

IT'S WHO YOU KNOW

Everyone says, "It's who you know." But it's not who you know. That's a lie. The truth is that it's what you *do*.

And the promise of what you can do doesn't always have to be spoken. It can be contained in your work, such as when a baseball scout says that a young player "shows promise," or when a rock group releases a "promising" first album. It's right there in the work.

In the world of success, who you know is nothing. What you *do* with who you know is everything. The *doing* is the thing that brings success.

For five years of my life I was a full-time songwriter. It was the hardest work I've ever done. For me, there was no more difficult way to make a living than to make it by trying to write a hit song. One had to write everything perfectly. Everything had to obey rhyme schemes and meter, and one had to have song titles and concepts that stood out above the millions of other songs vying for a recording artist's attention.

It was that degree of difficulty that made it so tempting to live by a lie. A lie like "it's who you know." The lie softened the blows.

I worked in the music business with the highly talented Fred Knipe. He and I invested a huge amount of our time in "it's who you know." We took trips, wrote letters, and made phone calls to expand our network of connections in the music business. We networked and schmoozed. When we were among groups of music executives, we worked the room. We got to know a lot of key figures on a lot of levels. And if there was ever time left over, we also wrote songs.

In the end, however, our biggest financial successes came from people who we did *not* know. In the end, networking meant nothing at all. The schmoozing was an empty waste of time and ego. Country singer Don Williams had a number one hit with Fred's *Listen to the Radio* and a popular album cut with Fred's and my *I Can't Get to You from Here*. But we didn't know him or anyone associated with him! Those songs were recorded because his producer had pulled our envelope out of a huge pile of unsolicited songs, played the songs, and fell in love with them. We didn't know him and he didn't know us. We didn't even know his address! We sent the songs to Don Williams' label address at Columbia Records. We got the address from an album cover, something any homeless person in any music store could have done.

After all those hours invested in networking, building relationships and making the right connections, it was *what we did* (in the writing of those songs) that the great producer Garth Fundis heard and converted into musical success. It wasn't who we knew; it was what we did.

"THE RIGHT SIDE OF THE WRONG BED"

As I look back on my five years in the songwriting business, I realize that it was always the best songs that actually went out there and found places to bloom. It wasn't who we knew, it was what we *did* when we wrote them. Fred and I wrote "The Right Side of the Wrong Bed" with Duncan Stitt, turned it loose, and watched it find its own places to bloom. It had nothing to do with our networking and schmoozing. It landed on a Mickey Gilley album, and then from that success, it seemed to find *its own way* onto Michael Landon's *Highway to Heaven* show.

Telling myself the lie that success depends on who you know was a deliberate attempt to avoid the real work of writing something extraordinary. It was an attempt to justify putting my time into easier, softer pursuits. Every time we lie to ourselves like this we are trying *not to go for it.*

It was this same lie, "it's who you know," that also kept me from writing books for many, many years. I always told myself that if you were an unknown writer and didn't know anybody in publishing, then you wouldn't have much of a chance in sending off an unsolicited manuscript somewhere.

Now that my first books have become fairly successful, it hurts to think back about how close I came to throwing it all away simply because I had talked myself into thinking that I didn't know anybody important enough to get things published.

I had been giving out a photocopied handout in my seminars called "21 Ways to Motivate Yourself," and because of the good response I always got from people who took the pamphlet home, I began to think that I might have the potential for a book in those twenty-one ways (especially when I began adding new ways in every course so that the number rapidly grew far beyond twenty-one).

But every time I thought about publishing a book, I ran up against the self-deceit that had always kept me out of action: "it's who you know!" I didn't know anyone in publishing. I didn't know any literary agents. I barely knew anyone in New York. I didn't have a chance.

Early one summer I was looking for some computer work for my daughter Stephanie to do. She wanted to earn money for summer camp, so I finally created a work project for her. I bought a book that listed all the publishers of books. It was the kind of book that I had always dismissed as being directed at the poor stupid people who didn't know how hard it was to get published.

I went through the book and picked out about sixty publishers who published nonfiction. I gave the book to Stephanie along with a letter to write to each publisher about my book-in-progress, *100 Ways to Motivate Yourself*. I gave her the "21 Ways to Motivate Yourself" handout to send with the letter of proposal to publishers. She went to work on the computer, writing each letter differently and tailoring each one to each particular publisher.

She worked long and hard, and I remember looking in on her as she sat at the computer in my home office late into the night. I thought that it was a little sad that this lovely fourteen-year-old girl was working so hard for nothing. This was just make-work.

Finally Stephanie was finished with her work, and sixty large envelopes were perfectly filled and addressed to the prospective publishers. I paid her for her efforts. She went off to her camp, saying to me, "Hey Dad that's going to be really neat to have a book out that's written by you!" I smiled and said, "Yes, that would be neat but we will have to see what the level of interest is because there are no guarantees."

Secretly I was thinking, "Poor thing. She doesn't know. She's naive. She doesn't realize that in the vicious dog-eat-dog world of publishing, it's not what you've got, *it's who you know.*"

So I put the sixty large envelopes in the back of my car and let them sit there for many days. I thought about the postage it would take to mail them all, and I began to think about simply disposing of them in a trash can. Stephanie wouldn't know. I'd explain when she got home from camp about how hard it is to get anything published. I came very close to throwing them all away.

START SPREADING THE NEWS

I remember when I was a small boy in Michigan, walking along the railroad tracks with my friend, Terry Hill, and seeing huge bundles of the shopping newspapers down by the tracks. "What are these?" I asked Terry. He said that people who had a shopping newspaper route would go to the tracks, throw their papers away, and then report them as delivered to collect their money. Back then I was shocked that someone could do that and live with themselves afterward. Now I realized that I was about to do the same thing. Newsboys were betraying the paper. I was about to betray myself.

So I couldn't make myself do it, not because of my own great character, but because of Stephanie. I could not forget that picture of her sitting there, late at night in her naivete working so hard to write all those letters. And I couldn't make myself throw the envelopes away. So I mailed them. "There goes nothing," I sighed as I drove away from the post office, believing I'd just wasted a lot of time and money.

And then it happened.

A little more than three weeks after I mailed the envelopes, the calls. First one publisher, then another. Some publishers were medium sized, some were very small, but some were large too! Doubleday called. Berkeley called. John

Wiley & Sons., and Career Press called. They liked the book idea and wanted to talk about publishing it. I was stunned and dumbfounded. In less than three weeks there were seven credible publishers who wanted the book. I was beside myself with joy. I thought back on all those years, ever since I was a little boy, when I walked through bookstores wondering what it would be like to have my own book in a store. And now it might really be happening.

It was hard to realize it was really happening because it went against my own self-authored truth: "It's who you know." As I had gotten older, I had begun to convince myself of how impossible my childhood dream of writing books would be. You had to have connections. Everyone knows that. Everyone tells you that.

But here were publishers calling. What was going on? In my joy, I called Stephanie at her camp in Michigan. She came to the phone out of breath from some game she'd been playing.

"Stephanie!" I said. "Guess what? You know those letters you worked on and the envelopes you made and all that?"

"Yes."

"Well! Guess what? I've got seven publishers interested in the book! Seven publishers who want the book! They called me, I didn't call them! Can you believe it?"

There was a long silence on the other end of the phone.

"Stephanie?" I asked.

The silence continued and then she said, "Only seven?"

I was at a loss for words. I hurried on to explain to her that even *one* publisher would be fine with me, and it's *hard* to get a book published if you . . . but then I shut up. I realized that I was furthering the lie. I realized that the very reason that the book was going to be published was because Stephanie had never been sold that lie, so I wasn't going to sell it to her now. I wished her well and she said good-bye and congratulations. Then she ran back to her game. The call was no surprise to her. She knew the book would be published because I had forgotten to teach her how impossible that would be.

*It takes a tremendous act of courage to admit to yourself
that you are not defective in any way whatsoever.*

—Cheri Huber,
*How You Do Anything Is
How You Do Everything*

THERE'S SOMETHING WRONG WITH ME

The great professor of linguistics S. I. Hayakawa said that there were basically two kinds of people: The kind of person who failed at something and said, "I failed at that" and the kind of person who failed at something and said, "I'm a failure."

The first person is telling the truth, and the second person is not.

"I'm a failure!"

That claim doesn't always appear to the outsider to be a lie. It can look like a sad form of self-acceptance. In fact, we can even associate such globalizing, such exaggerating, with truthful confession: "Why not admit it? I'm a failure."

However, it is a lie, and the lie is intentional. The payoff to this lie: If I am *already a failure,* how can I be criticized for not doing something great?

The consequences of this self-deception are huge. In *Cognitive Theories and Emotional Disorders,* psychiatrist Aaron Beck illuminates the consequences this way:

> His wife was upset because the children were slow in getting dressed. He thought, "I'm a poor father because the children are not better disciplined." He noticed that this showed he was a poor husband. While driving to work, he thought, "I must be a poor driver or other cars would not be passing me." As he arrived at work, he noticed some other personnel had already arrived. He thought, "I can't be very dedicated or I would have come earlier." When he noticed folders and papers piled up on his desk, he concluded, "I'm a poor organizer because I have so much work to do."

You can see what this man is doing to himself. He is taking innocent, meaningless situations and adding his own devastating meaning. He is turning them into indictments of himself. And because the sum of these unnecessary indictments causes him to believe that he is *defective*, he is killing his own spirit.

I used to do the same thing all the time. I used to tell myself that there was something wrong with me deep down inside. This kind of self-talk always kept me out of action. It removed all sense of purpose. That's what a lie to the soul is unconsciously designed to do.

There is some kind of voice in us, always in us, that says it's not *safe* to live on purpose. It's not safe to express yourself completely in the living of your true life. That's too big an adventure for someone who has something wrong. That's too big a risk for a defective person to take, the voice says. But the voice is the voice of a liar. It's the part of all of us that tries to lead us astray. It is the part that caused Scott Peck to write, in *The Road Less Traveled*, that laziness itself is the devil.

In psychological terms, the liar within is the voice of fear and passivity. It is the opposite of a soul purpose: a soul surrender. It is not to be confused with an external spanking: a defeat on the game board of life. But rather it is internal defeat: quitting before I begin.

Defeat and failure in the external world can actually be refreshing and rejuvenating. The great football coach Woody Hayes said, "Nothing cleanses the soul like getting the hell kicked out of you." But to claim defeat in the *internal* world of self-concept is to betray myself. And it begins by pretending that something is wrong with me.

One day, long ago when my children were very young, I was driving home from my job. I was not doing well financially at all. I had just checked my checking account and found that it was overdrawn. We had no groceries in the house at the time and I remember saying out loud to myself as I was driving along, "I don't have money for groceries. I can't even feed my own little children. I am such a failure that I can't even feed my children." Tears welled up in my eyes as I said that. I thought about how my failure was now going to affect my children. I drove over to my brother's place of business and borrowed fifty dollars from him to buy groceries with.

I was a failure, I said to myself. And at the time I could not admit that this was not the truth. The truth was that I could have stopped that lie right away. When I said that "I don't have money for groceries," I was correct. I should have stopped there and not gone on. That truth, "I don't have money for groceries," was a *useful* observation because it posed the problem clearly enough to derive an action plan from it. All problems can become action plans if we're willing to stay with them and follow the truth wherever it may lead.

I might have followed the truth in this direction: "Okay, so I need grocery money. Goal number one is to get enough money to buy groceries for two days for my family. I'll stop by my brother's. He'll loan it to me. Then I'll use that forty-eight hours of grace to *focus* all my energy on how to guarantee that I'll never be short of grocery money again. In fact, I'll turn this emotional little low into a lifelong high."

It was a lie to say that the shortage of money meant that I was a failure. I took a single isolated situation and tried to make it into a permanent exaggerated condition. Anytime I did that to myself, I was lying to my soul. I was killing my spirit and keeping myself trapped in a life of reaction to outside events. This just seemed to be the easiest way to live. A life of reaction feels like the easiest way to go. You just wake up and find out what rude surprises are waiting for you and then deal with those. That system of life takes no imagination. It takes no courage.

In those days, whenever I was losing my grip on a situation, I began writing it off to a permanent hardwired trait of my identity. That was convenient. Because it meant that I didn't have to boldly proceed in the direction of my dreams. What dreams? Eliminate dreams and you eliminate the "boldly proceed" part and that's the whole point. Individual incidents become overwhelming when they are filed in the brain this way. The truth was that I was out of grocery money. There was something wrong with *that*, but there was nothing wrong with *me*. I was making choices in life that led to my lack of money. But to say that there was something wrong with *me* is a lie that attempts to hide those choices. It is a lie that attempts to say that I am helpless. I am powerless due to some character defect. Action is not possible. Here is a little shotgun to help me sleep.

The truth is that no one is a failure. All people fail at certain things, but no one is a failure. To say so is to be as superstitious as calling some person a witch or demon. It is the same form of internal fear turned into an external label.

You've failed at some things, but there is nothing wrong with you. You are not defective. Not in any way whatsoever. It takes courage to hold on to this truth. But once you learn to hold on to it, it will give you your life back.

Whatever your age, your upbringing, or your education,
what you're made of is mostly unused potential.

—George Leonard,
Mastery

I'M TOO OLD
FOR THAT

One of the easiest ways for me to avoid doing something is to say that I'm too old to do it. It's a claim that keeps me out of action although it's almost never really *true* that I am too old to do it.

I don't want it to occur to me that it wasn't too long ago that I was telling myself that I was too *young* to do things, that I didn't really know *how* to yet. I didn't have enough experience or confidence.

These days I hear people say, "I'm too old for that" all the time. It becomes their way out of things. But it's almost never the truth. It's almost always just a feeling covered by an invented "fact." Should we honor and respect that feeling? Is feeling old a useful feeling?

◆   ◆   ◆

In his novel *Herzog*, Saul Bellow wrote, "Herzog experienced nothing but his own human feelings, in which he found nothing of use." And Horace Walpole said that this world is "a comedy to those that think and a tragedy to those that feel."

I have a friend who used to feel a lot. He felt a lot of frustration about his several careers that came close to making it but never quite did. And then finally, he began to *think:* What would I really *love* to be doing? Finally, he searched for *action* in the direction of his dream. Searching for action is what all our lies prevent.

My friend's name was Fred Knipe. Fred has always shared my assessment of professional comedy as the world's most underrated art form. I've been close to Fred for many years, and underneath all the friendship runs a solid line of pure comedic joy. When we were in basic training in the army together, I watched in wonder as he would keep the troops entertained with his ingenious imitations of the various drill sergeants' voices and mannerisms.

These days, Fred has been taking his most insanely amusing creation yet into the professional world with remarkably successful results. He has created a ludicrous character named Dr. M. F. Ludiker who is even funnier than Don Novello's Father Guido Sarducci. Dr. Ludiker is a "free-range scientist" with ridiculous opinions and offbeat erroneous theories on every subject under the sun.

The odd thing is this: Although he always was funny, turning it into a lucrative show business career didn't happen for Fred until he was fifty-two. But along the way, for a brief moment of hesitation, Fred confronted this horrible thought: What if it's too late? What if I'm too old to start a career as a professional comedian? Don't most people start in their twenties?

Then it hit him: *Only he* can decide if he's too old to do it. Only he can. When he decided that he wasn't, he wasn't. The beauty of exposing the way we lie to ourselves is that it frees us up to live on purpose. Lies burden the soul, and a person with a burdened soul lives randomly.

People who live in self-deceit will always tell you that they have a horrible feeling that they're not doing what they are supposed to be doing. They are not living their true lives. They say that circumstances have prevented them from being who they could really be. But was it circumstances? Or was it an exaggeration of the power of circumstances?

Fred has since told me that he believes we lie to ourselves to keep the soul from having an adventure. It is like trying to get an overly active child to go to sleep. Lying to the soul is like saying to the child, "You are too tiny to make a difference. Sleep now."

"I would love to hear you impersonate the liar," he said when I told him that I was going to write this book. "Impersonate the liar, singing to his own soul, like trying to get a child to stop chattering and go to sleep. In every chapter. Hush, little one, you are too beautiful for this world, here is a little shotgun for you to take to bed with you. It will help you sleep, my precious. Hush, hush, hush."

We even use the "I'm too old for that" lie to silence the learning process. We use it to hide and deny the truth that the mind needs to be worked to stay vital, quick, and strong.

Our current form of public education—kindergarten to high school to college—was designed in the Elizabethan Age, when humans had an average life expectancy of thirty-five years. For a person living thirty-five years, it was a sensible learning system that kept the mind alive and fresh for life.

But today, we have continued to use this educational structure despite having our average life span increase to seventy-five years. Our basic personal learning system is over when we are in our twenties. And yet we have over fifty more years to live.

Fortunately, many people have awakened to this problem. Some businesses have even instituted their own "universities" of learning to keep their employees mentally strong. I have worked as a visiting teacher at Motorola University and BGS University at U.S. West, and I am always impressed with the commitment to keep thought alive in these organizations. Without some kind of ongoing learning, the minds of humans grow soft, weak, and paranoid from a steady diet of television and Dilbert cartoons.

It's not your *age* that determines what you can learn, it's your energy. Your energy does not depend on your age, it depends on your sense of purpose. It comes from a self-generated sense of necessity: What needs to be done? And it comes from the actions taken as a result of that question.

WHIRL IS KING

I remember once conning myself into thinking that my age had put on a few extra pounds, that my age was the *cause* of the extra weight. (An old friend once said of another old friend that she wears big, shapeless dresses now "because she doesn't want the world to see too clearly what the ravages of time have done to her once youthful figure." The ravages of *time?*)

I wasn't unlike most people when I claimed that the *years* had added some inches to my waist. Despite this claim, I began reading books on weight loss and body fat. In one study, I read about metabolic set points. I learned that overweight people, because of their lower metabolic rate do subtle things to keep their weight where it is. There is a point, a level of metabolism, at which the body thinks it should be set.

For example, there was a study done of people's differences in energy when making a bed. The heavier the person, the more economy of movement he or she would exhibit in the making of the bed. They captured it on videotape. The heavy person would make the fewest and shortest movements around the bed, as if subconsciously trying not to exercise. The lighter person would move around and around the bed in a whirlwind of motion and movement. Therefore, the lighter person would expend more calories and burn more fat doing the *same* task. The point of the study, and of the hidden video in the bedroom, was to find out if we subconsciously conspire with our bodies to keep our weight from going down. It seemed to suggest that we do.

We secretly *try* to keep our body fat the same as it is and to keep our metabolic set point constant. Therefore, the trick to losing weight is to raise that set point by consciously overriding the subconscious system so that we burn more and more fat until our body assigns itself a new set point and a new weight.

But none of this can ever happen if we keep telling ourselves that we are too old to do something. It has to start there.

George Bernard Shaw thought that humans would one day learn to live three hundred years. He also thought that the key ingredient would be a more masterful use of the human mind, which would create a habit of continuously overriding and replacing the automatic perceptions of aging.

As we grow older, we tend to do just what the heavy people did when making their beds. In subtle and small ways, we start to cut down on motion and movement.

Whereas when I was younger I never used valet parking, I now enjoy the service. I don't notice that it eliminates a lot of small but significant exercise in my evening, as I now no longer walk all the way from the parking lot. I don't notice that when I use this service, I don't even open and close my own car door.

As we get older and more financially secure, we often hire people to do what we used to physically do ourselves. In school we would bound up the stairs all day, but now elevators become the only way to go. We are lifted up and down in buildings by machines so that our fat will be preserved intact.

Our children grow older and begin taking out the garbage for us. It's subtle, the falling away of small physical and mental efforts. But they do fall away all the same. All the while our muscles grow weaker in such small percentages that we don't notice. But when we *do* start to notice it, we just tell ourselves that we are growing *older*.

We are not growing older, we are simply growing weaker. We are suffering from lack of motion.

Not long ago I read a magazine article that said that a senator, although only sixty years old, constantly refers to himself as "The Geezer" to his family. "That is so endearing!" we were led to think. "What a self-effacing non-phony!" we were encouraged to believe. "The Geezer! Ha, ha, ha, ha, ha, ha, ha, ha! Oh, Dad, come on!"

But really you can see what he is subconsciously doing to himself. We all do it. And we should consider not doing it because we live into our pictures of ourselves. We're driven by our own self-concept.

When we were younger it was our youthful *activity* that made us strong, not our calendar years. For example, when we were younger we would laugh more, shout more, sing more, and stay up all night talking more. This activity developed our strong, vibrant vocal cords.

Older people speak to us with thin, reedy, pathetic voices, and we think it's because they are *old*. But it is not. It is because they are losing their voices by not using their voices. It's not an elderly thing, it's an inactivity thing.

I know older actors, singers, teachers, and coaches whose voices are still strong and pure. When you see an active seventy-three-year-old stage actress interviewed, she never has that thin, reedy, pathetic senior citizen voice. Her voice is rich, strong, and full of life. Jessica Tandy, acting in her eighties, had the vibrant voice range of a twenty-year-old woman.

MACHINES THAT LIFT ME HIGHER

To say that I am too old for a pickup game of basketball is a lie. To say that I am out of shape is the truth. To say that I am too old to play certain difficult guitar pieces that I used to play is a lie. To say that I am out of practice is the truth. To say that I am too old to take the stairs is a lie. To say that

I have grown weak is the truth. I have taken too many elevators. I've let machines carry me like a pharaoh to my floor.

This same "aging" process would also occur in young people if they stopped their activities. I remember seeing young astronauts on television news clips emerging from space capsules, barely able to walk after spending weeks floating around weightlessly. The weightlessness removed all necessity for the leg muscles to function, so they grew weak.

Even a young boy whose arm is in a cast for a month will notice that the arm has shriveled to a smaller size than his other arm and is now weak. It would not occur to him to say that his arm had become old.

The "I'm too old for that" lie is a way of deliberately avoiding this truth: *Use it or lose it.*

Recent experiments done in nursing homes with elderly patients have surprised researchers. Many patients who were thought to be wheelchair-bound for life (because of advanced age) became mobile and strong again after lifting weights.

As the average life span of a human being, which not too many generations ago was just thirty-five years, keeps increasing toward Shaw's three hundred years, we are discovering that the aging process, while certainly a reality, was greatly exaggerated for its debilitating effect on human energy.

AND A RIVER RUNS THROUGH IT

We do the same thing with our mental activity. The same *use it or lose it* dynamic is as important to the brain as it is to our muscles. What we used to attribute to senility is now being discovered to often be a simple lack of use. As we get older, we do less and less thinking. We hire accountants, lawyers, and assistants to think for us. Our love of books gives way to the remote control and mindless viewing. We begin the downward slide. It's a slippery slope once we sit down on it. Because the less thinking we do the less we *can* do.

People who work crossword puzzles in old age keep their brains and memories sharper and *even live longer* than do those who spend time in front of the life-devouring television set.

At the age of seventy-three, Norman Maclean decided to reject the idea of going into a comfortable retirement. It would have been easy to do. He had taught literature at the University of Chicago for many years, and he "deserved" a nice, restful retirement. But something was nagging him. In all the years that he taught literature he wondered if he himself could have been a writer. Then he took the great writer George Eliot's advice: "It's never too late to be what you might have been."

Norman Maclean said he "decided to give up some of the things associated with happiness in old age like running around with women, travel, etcetera." Instead, he would find out if he could be a writer. He went to his cabin in Montana and, in a joyfully disciplined way, began to write. He realized that he had it right there in his hands to experience his true life. Two years later he emerged with his highly acclaimed masterpiece, *A River Runs Through It*. It is a novel written with a passion and poetic fire normally only associated with young brains. It was simply *not true* that he was too old to become a writer.

Yet I can't tell you how many people have told me that they "always wanted to be a" writer, actor, musician, or something like that, but that now of course, it was a little late because they were thirty or forty or fifty years old. "I'm too old for that," they say with a straight face.

Lying about age is done to hide what is true about action. It is true to the soul that action is always possible in the direction of one's dreams. Avoiding effort is fine if I permit myself to know what I'm doing. If I take the elevator instead of the stairs, it's perfectly all right so long as I am conscious of what I am really doing. If I pretend that the resultant loss of muscularity in my legs is because of aging, I am not being straight.

Man is the only animal who has to be encouraged to live.
—Friedrich Nietzsche,
Thus Spake Zarathustra

I CAN'T
BECAUSE I'M
AFRAID

I am afraid to do it," I would always say to myself. And then I would believe that if I were *afraid* to do something, that was the same as not being *able* to do it.

"Are you going to do that, Steve?"

"No. I can't. I'm afraid to."

There was a bully in my first grade who was larger than I was. Somehow he could sense that I was afraid of being in school (I was afraid of being anywhere without my mother), so he decided to play upon that fear and see just how afraid he could make me. This guy whom I will call Charlie was like the killer on the road whose brain was squirming like a toad that Jim Morrison sang about in "Riders on the Storm." Maybe Charlie believed that the more afraid he could make me the better he himself would feel. As long as he was terrifying someone, he could not at that very moment be terrified.

But what happened to me was that I took Charlie seriously. Like some people really create a virtual Satan after thinking about him long enough, I did the same with Charlie. I scripted mental software about Charlie that said I was, deep down inside of me, someone who could be paralyzed with fear. Paralyzed, fearing not only fear itself but fearing fear itself so fiercely that my *whole life* became absolutely frightening. I almost longed for something *real* to come along, like a big Michigan tornado, that frightened *everyone* so that I could just feel fear along with everyone else and test whether it was true that I felt fear more than others.

Charlie found me again and again in the hallways and on the playground. He looked at me, and he threatened me. He was going to hurt me in ways I'd never been hurt. Back then it never occurred to me how badly Charlie himself must have been shaken up by someone to treat me this way. I thought it was something in *me*. In my dreams, Charlie appeared as a large boy with a dog's head on him, an inhuman thing, outright evil, twisting and reeking of the stench of cruelty. I began fearing my dreams of Charlie at night. In them I would be looking out of the window of my home, way down the road at Charlie in a trench coat with a dog's head on top, who ducked away when *it* saw me.

I was a *coward*. That's what I programmed into my bio-computer at the time: you coward. ("I don't have what it takes. I don't have it in me to stand up to this.") I then collected numerous forms of evidence to confirm the "truth" of that. I was always afraid of getting hurt. They were going to hurt me. *It* was going to hurt me.

Tony Buzan and Michael Gelb talk about our inordinate fear of getting hurt in their book *Lessons from the Art of Juggling*. You and I begin our lives as fearless beings and then get re-programmed:

Masters of trial-and-error learning, babies fall repeatedly. They do it in a relaxed, almost comfortable manner, making it unlikely that they will be harmed. Anxious parents, however, often induce shock or fear reactions in the child by communicating their *own* fear about what the baby is doing ("Oh my God! you will *hurt yourself!*").

And it doesn't matter if later in life there is evidence to the contrary of this "you'll hurt yourself" programming. Once the lie is repeated long enough, it's your new truth.

In the fifth grade, there was a boy my age who was the most fearless athlete in our neighborhood. I'll call him Jimmy. He was taunting me for something or other, and for some unknown reason my brain fused, all fear left me, and I punched him. I decked him with a furious blow to his jaw that left him sprawled on the ground. I looked into his eyes, and they were huge. He was temporarily very scared of what had just happened. I quickly walked home, not wanting to continue this physical exchange, and neither of us ever spoke of it again. Later I would read of his prowess as an all-state linebacker who was physically reckless and feared no one.

Even though I had decked him, my biocomputer would not let that incident become new evidence of anything. Even though I did something I was afraid to do, I still culti-vated the lie that if I was afraid to do something, then I could not do it. My brain already made up its program and script. The knockdown punch was deliberately dismissed as an anomaly, a mistake. It was a fluke. One of those lucky sucker punches you read about. A phantom shot like Ali against Sonny Liston.

But was it? Couldn't it have been what William Butler Yeats was talking about when he wrote about completing the partial mind:

> When a man is fighting mad
> Something drops from eyes long blind
> He completes his partial mind.

When conscious and subconscious fuse rapidly, the left side of the brain shouts to the right, "Drop this guy! You can do it! Now!" When fused together, I become Superman. I complete my partial mind. Bring on Charlie.

Once I was willing to give up the "I'm a total coward" act, I could talk to myself differently. I became something like my own parent. I did some essential reparenting and told my inner boy that Charlie was the coward, not me. And that if Charlie had pushed me one inch further, I would have crushed his jaw, broken his nose, and sent him home crying to his mother. The true me was the one who floored Jimmy with one punch. That was the true self below the lie. I could always draw on that self when I wanted to.

The truth is that every human has as much courage as the current purpose requires. Courage is always in us, like a heartbeat, like breath. It's in all of us in equal measure. To say we don't have it is to lie. It's to deliberately generate a horrible superstition, a vision of fear, a vision of a human with an animal's head. The lie keeps us from being bold. It keeps us from bravely striking out in the name of our dignity. If we exaggerate the fear, we can claim that it has immobilized us. Why aren't you taking action? "I am paralyzed with fear" is the claim. It's a claim made to forgive inactivity.

My own son, Bobby, doesn't have the same fear of getting hurt that I had at his age. In fact, in my own painful awareness of how false programming can happen, I have been acutely aware, maybe even to a fault, of how my children deal with physical fear.

For example, I always encouraged Bobby to fall and take his tumbles. He enjoyed it so much that as he got a little older, he turned it into a stage act that would horrify friends and relatives. As a little boy no more than four years old, he would love taking dramatic pratfalls like a tiny stuntman. What he loved most was watching grown-ups shriek and panic as he stood on a chair and tipped backward, rotating his arms in a pinwheeling motion while yelling "Whoa! Whoa! Whooooooa!" Then he would fall to the floor and pretend to be out cold. When people gathered around him (I was never among them) he would sit up laughing like a cute little maniac, annoying everyone but me. I knew what he was doing. He was showing me what my own childhood could have been. I loved it because by then I realized that you can live your childhood again, not through your children, but inspired by them all the same. Little Bobby was the opposite of me! I was so timid when I was young that I actually looked at people in wheelchairs longingly. That would be so safe.

Today I watch Bobby play basketball like a boy possessed. He is thirteen years old, and when he gets the fire in his soul he rebounds in a fury, knocking bodies down as he tears the ball off the backboard. I watch him with a sense of wonder because when I was his age, I also played basketball, but I didn't play like Bobby. I played guard and made certain that I got through each game with as little physical contact as possible. In fact, my best shot was a baseline fadeaway jumper that ended with me actually going out of bounds after launching the shot. Out of bounds and beyond the field of play. I didn't enjoy being in bounds. That's where the players were. And they were aggressive.

I don't know what finally became of Charlie. But I do know that Charlie would not stand a chance with me today.

He wouldn't even stand a chance with that "inner child" (the memory cluster in my brain that recalls the feelings of the little boy) inside of me. Because I can talk to that child now. I can grow him up. I can show him the moves to use on Charlie.

The self-concept of cowardice brings about the lie that being afraid to act is being unable to act. The truth is that I can always find courage. It's right there inside the fear! It's like a jewel inside a closed fist. It is not something I don't have. It's not a missing gene.

Courage reveals itself in action. "See?" says the courage. "I was always here for you. I am always here for you. I am a basic part of who you really are."

Life is never exhausted because it is pure potentiality.

—Colin Wilson,
Beyond the Occult

I'D LOVE TO DO THAT, BUT I DON'T HAVE THE TIME

There's never enough time!" You will hear that right after you've heard, "I really want to do that, but I don't have the time."

Neither is true. It is not true that they really want to do that, and it is not true that they don't have the time. If they really wanted to do that, they would make the time. There is always enough time. It is never time that people lack, it is always purpose.

So it would be more honest to say, "I think I should say I want to, but I don't have the commitment."

Desires, when they are strong, can be converted into clear commitments. And then pure enthusiasm causes the *creation* of time. Soon there's lots of time. When the desire is strong, we have all the time in the world.

When I work as a business consultant and corporate trainer, I see people become weak, professionally, from trying to work on too many things. Things they think they should want to do. Then they become even weaker by trying to think about too many things. Soon they are going too fast from thing to thing as if they were playing a wild game of tag. They are just barely tagging, quickly touching everything, running away from it, back to it, and then away from it to something else. They screw up their businesses by not taking time to pay attention to any one thing.

For many years, this had been my own problem in my professional life. I ran from one job to another like a kid at his first carnival, jumping on the tilt-a-whirl, running over to the rifle range, getting on the Ferris wheel, jumping off before it stopped, and running through half the house of horrors before crawling out a trap door in the bottom to scramble toward the cotton candy booth before they sold out. That was my professional life. In a way, it made things interesting (especially to the IRS). But soon it got too chaotic to support, especially with children growing into it.

In those days, I simply tried to think of too many things every day. And by thinking of too many things every day, I never gave anything enough time or real thought to develop it. I wish I had known to tell myself this: Slow down. Do less. Accomplish more.

Someone asked Sir Isaac Newton, "How did you discover the theory of gravity?" He said, "You would have discovered it too if that's all you had thought about every day."

That was my problem. I never chose the one thing I wanted to get great at, so I never got great at anything. I wrote songs for a few years, and some of them were good songs that got made into good records, but I was too impatient with the profession to take the time to be great. Even when semi-famous people recorded the songs, my mind was always racing ahead of itself, trying to get rich. I never stopped to really write. I never settled into my life. I was always on the mental run.

I didn't realize that the real strength in life came from slowing down and slowly choosing what to focus on. Until I saw how strong that idea could be, I was taking every phone call and pondering every piece of mail with equal energy. That is definitely weak. That is not a strong way to live.

Roy Evernham, the highest-rated crew chief in NASCAR (National Association for Stock Car Racing) once worked for racing superstar Jeff Gordon. Evernham's motto is "To speed up, slow down."

"I still have to prove this principle to Jeff sometimes," said Evernham. "I'll say, 'Go out and bust me a lap.' He'll drive the car hard, really work it. He'll mash the pedal on a straightaway, drive down into a corner, and mash the pedal again. Then I'll say, 'Now, take it easy and drive a smooth lap.' And by letting the car do the work, he actually improves his time."

One slow thing at a time is a strong way to live. Being focused is a strong way to live.

Richard Sloma explains it better than I do in his powerful book *No-Nonsense Management:*

Pardon the cliché, but General Custer could have become one of our most famous military heroes if, somehow, he could have forced the Sioux nation to attack over the hill one at a time. Supremacy of the seas was guaranteed for the British when Lord Nelson maximized and exploited the technique of "crossing the 'T'" so as to allow all of his ships to fire broadside at each enemy ship as it appeared next in line. Look at problems as adversaries. Summon all your forces and deal with them one at a time.

A few years ago, I was complaining to my consultant and coach, Steve Hardison, that I was overwhelmed. I was swamped. I had so many problems and challenges pressing me that I didn't know what to do.

He walked into my office and saw the clutter on my desk. He said, "Are you willing to try something? As an experiment?"

"Sure," I said.

He then walked over to my desk and picked up the piece of paper that was on top of the pile by my phone.

"You have only one problem in life," he said.

"Only one?" I asked.

"Yes," he said, handing me the paper. "This problem. It's the only problem you've got. Take care of this problem."

"Well!" I said, "What about all the others?"

"Forget them for the moment. It's thinking about them that has stopped you from handling this one. Handle this one, and then pick up another one. Only think of one at a time, but stay in action. Be completely focused on the one problem you are working on. Bring everything you've got to it. Focus all your resources on that one problem, and keep reminding yourself, *this is all I've got,* so that you can bring your most creative effort to it. You won't hold anything back that way."

"But what if I'm working on the wrong thing?" I said. "What if I should really be working on something else?"

"Just do it," he said. "The trouble you're having with your life is not that you might be working on the wrong thing, the trouble is that *you're not really focused on anything.* Once you completely clear this office out, one problem at a time, we'll get together and talk about the other subjects. Priorities. Commitments. Your invented future. We'll look at which of your problems shouldn't have been there in the first place. For now, just handle them, and remember to do them all with the thought that you only have *one problem* to solve."

Steve's coaching matched exactly with Richard Sloma's ideas. The reason Custer was defeated was because he was swamped. He was overwhelmed. The Sioux were too bold and creative to come at him in single file, one at a time. If he could have gotten them to line up that way, he could have taken them out quite easily. We *can* get our problems to line up that way because we are in charge of our time.

The reason Lord Nelson was so successful was that he had his own ships line up sideways to form a "T" with the enemy coming single file over the horizon. As each enemy ship appeared, Nelson's ships all fired *at that one ship only.* So even when both sides had the same number of ships, Nelson's side always won because it was *all against one.* When we line up all the resources of our mind against a single problem, we create that same all-against-one advantage. Problems are then solved quickly and creatively, sometimes with brutal speed.

When I lie about time, I become an enemy of time. Time is against me. It's running out. There's never enough! However, when I forget time and focus on my one problem instead, time is all of a sudden on my side again. Time is my ally. It is the stuff of which life is made.

The only reason you suffer is because you choose to suffer.
—Don Miguel Ruiz,
The Four Agreements

THERE'S
NOTHING I
CAN DO

Every day I used to wake up to the idea that maybe my spirit would fire up on its own. Or that maybe a movie, good book, or inspirational conversation would fire it up.

And then financial, familial, or professional circumstances were ignored long enough to push me into various corners that I had to fight my way out of. Soon the crisis itself fired me up. And it became a habit. To find energy, I would just wait for a crisis to get big enough.

Before the crisis hit, when thinking about any problem area of my life, I would just tell myself, "There's nothing I can do." By saying that, I didn't ever have to think any further about the problem.

I had not yet accepted that I had control over my life. I hadn't faced the fact that I didn't have to wait for external pressure to force me into action. I didn't want to face the truth that I could create my own internal pressure.

Today I often return to six simple words to put me back in touch with that pressure. I take this quotation and repeat it a lot. I even repeat it to other people. I don't mind it when people respond that I've already told them it. Because some quotes, some ideas, are so useful that they actually get *stronger* for you each time you say them.

Just such a quote for me is this one by Henry David Thoreau:

"Things do not change. We change."

Things do not change. We change! If that's really true, why do we waste our precious lives wishing things would change? Why spend so much time hoping things will be different?

"Most of us never make it beyond adolescent hope and hype and disappointment," says psychotherapist Dr. Brad Blanton. "Wishing is a way to remove oneself from what is going on now. Hope springs eternal. I say @#!*! hope. Hope is how most of us avoid growing up."

NOTHING SUCCEEDS LIKE FAILURE

Lying to the soul is an unconscious attempt to avoid changing. We lie by telling ourselves, "People never change, I'll never change. That's how it is. There's nothing I can do."

But there's always something I can do. And if what I do fails, so what? It has changed *me* just to do something, just to be in action instead of checking out and curling up.

Another quote is useful right here. It's from G. K. Chesterton, who said, "Nothing succeeds like failure."

Most of us have an irrational, superstitious fear of failure. We think it would be awful if we tried something and it didn't "work," if we tried something and failed. Failing would be worse, we think, than not trying anything.

But when we say that "it might not work," what we really mean is that "it might not change things." But that's forgetting that "Things do not change. We change." So my trying and failing might not change the external thing, but it could change the internal thing: my own sense of control.

Nothing succeeds like failure. The man who created the company known as IBM, Thomas Watson Sr., said, "If you want to double your success rate, double your failure rate."

It is fear of failure that prevents success. It is fear of losing that causes a team not to win. I once watched a local university lose the Rose Bowl by putting in every possible overcoached fearful precaution known to football in the final moments of the game, out of terror that they would lose their lead. A cautious short kickoff. A timid deep-zone defense, etcetera. All it did was take the spirit out of the team right when they were lusting to go in for the kill. All it did was focus every player on the *fear* that they might lose. It was a major transfer of fear from the coaching staff to the players.

Just like a parent does to a baby. A baby is a soft bundle of supple bone and flesh and can fall and fall again without getting hurt. That's how the baby learns to walk and then run and then rush for a touchdown.

But the parent sees the baby about to fall and screams out, "No! No! No! You might *hurt* yourself!" As if hurting yourself is always a bad thing. What occurs is a transfer of fear. It starts a way of life called "playing not to lose."

The great basketball coach John Wooden would say to his team before a game, "The team that makes the most mistakes today will win."

I was waiting in line at a bookstore recently, and the elderly gentleman in front of me was making a request of the woman behind the counter.

"You get the *Wall Street Journal*, don't you?" he asked her.

"Yes," she said somewhat impatiently.

"Well, I won't be coming into the store until tomorrow afternoon, and I wonder if you could hold tomorrow's *Wall Street Journal* for me?"

"We don't really have any way of doing that," she said.

"You can't save one for me?" he asked.

"No sir, there's nothing in our system that would allow us to do that."

"It doesn't seem like it would be too hard to . . ."

"Sir, I just told you, *there's nothing I can do!*"

As I witnessed this pathetic little scene I wondered if it were true that there was nothing she could do. I could think of one thing immediately: she could take his name and make sure that when the *Wall Street Journal* came in, one was set aside for him with his name on it. She could even ask him to prepay for it. I began to think of many other things she could do if she wanted to. But it was obviously *easier* for her to lie to herself and to him. There's nothing I can do. That's always a lie.

If *you* worked there, you'd buy him a paper yourself. You would go to a store across town if your store ran out. You'd do anything you had to, to get it done. You either serve in life, or you don't serve. There is no gray area. If your commitment is to serve, then there's always something you can do.

I also began to think about how much money that old gentleman had spent at her store over the past few years. Why would it seem better to lie to him than to honor him? Lying to him was just an outer symptom of the lying she had to be doing to herself: "There's nothing I can do about this job. There's nothing I can do about these unreasonable customer demands. There's nothing I can do about being happy at work and having a fulfilling career."

This was a bookstore that had done a lot to make itself appear warm and user-friendly. It had even created a little coffeehouse so that patrons could sip espresso the way the beatniks used to do while discussing books. It had a piano upstairs where performers played cool jazz to further enhance the atmosphere. "Come on in, cool people, hunch over your coffee like desolation angels." That was the message.

Yet they couldn't hold a newspaper for a little old man who wanted one badly. When he walked away sadly, and it was my turn in line, I said to the lady who had turned him down that I had just changed my mind. I would return these books to the shelves and buy them off the Internet. I would not be back. I told her why.

There's always something I can do.

To worry is to pray for what you don't want.

—Dr. Deepak Chopra,
Journey to the Boundless

I WORRY
BECAUSE I CARE

The man looked very worried as he approached me after I had concluded one of my seminars. He looked like he could barely bring himself to talk to me.

"Do you need a break?" he asked.

"I don't really," I said. "These subjects are so stimulating that it's hard to just stop talking about them, so I'm glad to talk to you. Thanks for coming up."

"Well, I probably shouldn't be saying this because I sound like a victim, maybe, but I'm really worried about my mother," he said. "She's so negative about everything. I'm worried my own children have inherited that too. And my wife's not much help with any of this, which is why I worry, sometimes, about this marriage and how I can make it last."

"Why are you worried about your mother?" I asked.

"Well! She's so negative about everything. She's a pessimist, and she doesn't do much of anything anymore, and I think she should go out. Or join a group or volunteer for something."

"Why does it matter to you?"

"Because I care!"

"You care about your mother and what she does."

"Yes, that's right. I care. I worry because I care."

"Have you taken her to any groups? Any volunteer groups that you want her to join? Have you taken her there?"

"No, I'm worried that she won't go. She'll take it wrong if I suggest it."

"Have you had a real straight heart-to-heart talk with her?"

"Not really. She doesn't take very kindly to those. She says I should live and let live. She says I should let her live any way she wants."

"What if I were to disagree with you about something right now? Would that be okay with you?"

"Well, yes, of course! That's why I wanted to talk to you."

"Okay then, thank you for your courage. So I will suggest this as a possibility. See if it fits. I don't need to be right. I'm just trying to make us think at a higher level about all this."

"Go ahead!"

"Consider this possibility: We don't worry about our mothers because we care about our mothers. We worry because worrying is *what we do* all day to avoid taking action. We worry because we're in the habit of worrying. That's how we occupy our minds. It's a habit. We worry because we worry because we worry. It has become an activity that we can't get out of our heads. Like those songs that get on the jingle track of our brains and we can't get them out for days. It seems like worrying has become your theme song."

He nodded his head and smiled. I could see that he wasn't going to resist that possibility. We talked for a long time about worrying as a habit, and in as gentle a way as I could, I finally got him to see that it's not really true that he worries because he cares.

He worries because he doesn't have any action to take. And on a deeper level, he worries because he doesn't have a life of his own, at least not in the sense that his life is intriguing and exciting enough to him to make other people's habits no big deal.

If we have a life of our own, we will not be worried about other people living up to our expectations. If we saw something missing in them and found an opportunity to contribute, we might be in action, but we wouldn't be worrying. We would be *doing* something about it. We would be driving our mother to the meeting of volunteers and introducing her to the people we had met there. We would be telling those people all about our mother, all the good things. All the things we were proud of her for. We'd be bragging like crazy. And as soon as possible we would leave her alone with them because they would also come to love her.

I have a foolproof piece of advice for the chronic worrier. I promise you this will work. For the next two weeks, take immediate notice of every time you worry. When you catch yourself worrying—take an action. Any action, but make sure you take one. Do something. Anything. And remember, you *must* do something every time you worry. This is a great way to train yourself not to worry, especially if you hate being in action.

The truth is not that "I worry because I care." The truth is that "I worry because I am in the habit of worrying." I worry in order to do nothing. Doing nothing about a problem soon *becomes* the problem. As Wayne Gretzky said, "You miss 100 percent of the shots you don't take."

A sad soul can kill you quicker, far quicker, than a germ.

—John Steinbeck,
Travels with Charley

I'M SADDER
NOW
BUT WISER

People often take on sadness as a way of being because it is so easy and feels like the safest way to be. No one can stifle your enthusiasm if you don't have any.

But then people begin to lie about it. They say that they are sad because they are wise. They say that they are sad because they have seen so much, and they understand so much. This lie not only forgives them for the weakness of their sad way of being, but it attempts to make a virtue of it. It attempts to say sadness comes from wisdom, so it is not weak or deliberate.

But a sad way of being is weak. And it is a very deliberate act. It is a form of playing dead.

On the battlefield in war, many men have saved their lives by playing dead. Enemy patrols would stroll through the smoking, bleeding aftermath of a battle and shoot anything that moved. Those who played dead often lived to fight another day.

And it struck me one day while sitting in a company meeting how many of us in that room were playing dead. Keeping a low profile, like soldiers lying on the battlefield of the meeting, letting the daring few people carry the day. I studied the faces in the room during that meeting, and I noticed that many were looking thoughtful and somewhat sad. I had an impulse to pull a calculator from my folder and see if I could calculate how many hours a week we spend *not* being excited. How many sad hours do we run up? How many would you guess that would be? I wished I could somehow go back in time and pick a day at random when I was five years old and calculate how much of *that* day was spent not being excited. Probably less. Probably a lot less. It would be an interesting comparison.

I then looked around the same meeting room. It struck me that looking a little sad bore a remarkable resemblance to looking mentally slow. I saw an eerie connection between sadness and stupidity that gave me goose bumps and stayed with me from that moment on. I realized that to take on this cover of sadness, we have to dim ourselves a bit. We have to dumb down our minds to be disappointed with life and people. We have to get a little idiotic.

But the irony seemed to be this: People were appearing to be stupid so that they would not risk *looking* stupid. They had safe reputations to protect, and they didn't want to spoil it all by saying something stupid like, "I *love* that!"

I then thought of how these people must be lying low *everywhere* in their lives. I was tempted to stand up in the meeting and shout out, in the words of the Zen writer Cheri Huber, "How you do anything is how you do *everything*!"

LET'S PLAY DEAD SO LIFE DOESN'T SHOOT US

In my notebook, during this particular company meeting, I wrote the words, "Being chronically sad is being chronically slow, like sad Stan's face in Laurel and Hardy. Not being excited is to have missed the whole point of life." It wasn't long before the meeting was over. I remember leaving it thinking that I had gotten a lot out of it. Inside that very meeting, it was pretty clear to me that people were playing dead so life wouldn't shoot them.

Since that revealing meeting, I've had many, many occasions to sit in other company meetings. I sometimes serve as a consultant, showing people or groups of people possibilities for reinventing themselves. These meetings have given me firsthand knowledge of what other people refer to as near-death experiences. I can tell you quite truthfully that there were times when a company leader's talk to his team was so bland and boring that I felt the hair stand up on the back of my neck. People would later say to me, "What happened to you in there? You looked like you had seen a ghost."

And even though the leader might be outspoken and upbeat in another setting, what he was generating in his company felt as cold and evil as the darkest Dean Koontz novel. His deliberate avoidance of enthusiasm sent a clammy, moist chill through the room.

(The word "enthusiasm" comes from the Greek *en theos*, which means "the God within." If that's what enthusiasm means, you can figure out what the opposite of enthusiasm is.)

Sometimes during those meetings, I would see if I could stir things up. I would deliberately inject something wild or controversial into the proceedings to stimulate and polarize the room. To stir the pot or fire off a few brain cells that were on their way to the morgue.

AM I LIVING AS A HAPPY IDIOT?

Sometimes I sit down and stare at the earnest suicidal sadness of the evening news anchor explaining the melancholy results of a poll just taken on how America has reacted sadly to the public opinion polls of last week. If I become sufficiently weary of the anchor, I click over to the effete, sophisticated nihilism of his counterpart on another network, who will demonstrate that nothing in the world today had any inspiration or beauty in it, with the possible exception of the colorful tie he is now wearing.

Then it happens. I get the surge I wanted. My mind is finally off its *ass* and thinking. The news anchor's sad face illustrates an important *lie* that I had been telling myself all my life: "I'm a sadder man but wiser now."

I had eagerly bought into the false idea that sadder and wiser *go together*, that they progress along the same lines, that someone who does not understand that is living as a happy idiot. But it is simply *not true* that sadder and wiser are related to each other!

The old folk song about the lemon tree got the lie started in my head when I was young. In the song, the singer's lover leaves him.

> One day she left without a word
> she took away the sun
> and in the dark she left behind
> I knew what she had done
> she left me for another
> it's a common tale but true
> a sadder man but wiser now
> I sing these words to you

A sadder man but wiser now, I sing these words to you. The lesson of the lemon tree is this: the lemon tree is very pretty, as is life itself. But once you bite into it, watch out. You're in for a bitter surprise. Bite into that pretty lemon fruit and you learn a bitter lesson. A sadder man but wiser now, you can sing the evening news.

The lesson is a lie.

The real truth is that the wiser you are, the *happier* you get. Because wisdom does that. If one is becoming sadder, it's not because one is becoming wiser, it is because one is *quitting*. One is giving up. She left me for another, so I quit. When a bitter Bob Dylan sings in a self-pitying voice, "I'm sick of love," it's not really *love* he's sick of. It's the victim game that people play when they are not wise enough to really love each other.

Sadder and wiser don't match. The truth is that when I am getting wiser, I am getting happier. I am learning to love the kind of person who would not leave me for another. I don't bite into the lemon. I might use the lemon for other things. That's the joy of wisdom, and it doesn't make me sad.

Wisdom implies growth. It implies a warm and friendly gathering of awareness of and insight into how the universe works. The more I know about how something works, the happier I am to be with it. The more I know about the universe, the happier I am to be in it. Look at the joy of physicists Albert Einstein and Richard Feynman, who knew more about the universe than anyone.

People who are happiest at their computers are people who know the most about what they can' do on their computers. People who are happiest about working on a car are the ones who know the most about cars. The happiest fan at the game is the one who follows the team most completely.

WE'RE ADDICTED TO BEING VICTIMS

If it were true that you got sadder as you got wiser, the human race would have committed suicide long ago. To keep selling myself the "sadder but wiser" lie, I have to assume that the universe is basically a depressing place to live, that the moon and the stars will let me down. The truth is, however, they won't ever let anyone down. They are too beautiful to do that. That's what the wise person can see. That's what the sad person does not want to see.

"We're addicted to being victims," writes Cheri Huber in her marvelous book *That Which You Are Seeking Is Causing You to Seek.* "We are so privileged that we have to ignore vast areas of our lives in order to pick out those things that aren't the way we want them to be. This process of ignoring and selective perception lets us continue to see ourselves as victims of circumstances."

A victim's sadness will spread like a rumor. I remember visiting my daughter Margery when she was a newborn in the hospital. I'd go stare at her in the nursery in there with all those other babies. I'd be looking through the glass, and I would see a strange event. One baby would start to cry, and then others, hearing that baby, would start to cry too. Pretty soon the whole room of babies was crying. It had spread.

I see this same kind of spreading going on in companies too. Sadness spreads like a frightening superstitious piece of news. There's a bad moon out tonight, pass it on. People deliver bad news, and the news of the bad news starts to spread.

Managers often kick this off by telling their teams that "change" is bad news, and that there will be more changes coming. And you can see the sadness start to spread. Managers apologize for the changes. They apologize for the competition in the global market. And then they bring out the saddest word of them all: *cope.* They say that we are going to have to learn to *cope* with the changes.

I give seminars for a living. Sometimes though, company managers ask me to come in and deliver a seminar on the subject of "coping with change." I refuse to deliver such a seminar. It is a defeated idea from the beginning. It can only encourage company-wide self-pity.

THE LIGHT AT THE END OF THE UNIVERSE

And I listen to these people who want to learn to "cope with change," and I wonder about the choice of the word "cope." Isn't that a word you use with terminal illness?

"Mr. Chandler, your illness is such that you have now lost control of all your bodily functions. It's irreversible. All you can do is learn to cope with it, but Nurse Allright will be here right away to help you cope with your new situation."

We do this in our families too. Anything different and unaccustomed is sad. It's sad that we're being transferred to another city. We have to move. That's sad. It's sad that Stephanie is going to college next year. It's sad that your father's brother won't talk to him anymore. What else is sad? Our neighbors are moving away? (Didn't we hate them?) We're getting a new area code? Anybody have anything else? Bobby? Oh! Your teacher is out and you have to have a substitute for a week? That's sad. Sadness swarms in and smothers the soul. Unnecessarily manufactured sadness prevents us from living our true lives.

In Cheri Huber's book there is a cartoon of a woman with her head hung low, and on her shirt are the words, "Sad but Safe." Being a sad victim feels safe even though it's based on self-deceit. When we lie to ourselves often enough it feels safer than the truth does.

However, in reality it's not safer. Lies are never safer because they blind us to our options for action. We misunderstand all we see. The lies then hide what's possible. But we think that we can live inside the lies because we are used to them. We've told them so often that they feel like home.

It's the truth that we've become afraid of. The truth is this: Sadder and wiser *do not* go together. The truth is that we get happy when we get wise, and we don't even let ourselves know it! We're always much happier than we think. We only feel unhappy with what we've got until someone tries to take it away from us.

We still haven't completely integrated what Ral Donner was trying to teach us: "You don't know what you've got until you lose it."

Sadness comes from dimming the lights, not turning them up. Sadness comes from *not* wanting to know, not wanting to think about it, not lighting up the mind.

Happiness, on the other hand, comes from being progressively wiser, from brightly lighting our consciousness with new knowledge and power. If knowledge is power (and in this day and age it surely is), then fresh knowledge is *added* power. It is the *surge* at the stem of the brain that we all love to feel.

A "sadder man but wiser now" is lying to his soul.

Beaten people take beaten paths.

—George Matthew Adams

THE LONGER I HAVE A HABIT, THE HARDER IT IS TO BREAK

People have habits that they want to break, but because they don't want to take the action necessary to break them, they begin to lie about their habits. They lie to *themselves*, which is the deepest and most damaging kind of lie because it stops all chance of real change.

For example, people will tell themselves that "I've had this habit too long to even consider letting go of it. Everybody knows that the longer you have a habit, the harder it is to break."

Everybody may know that, but it is not the truth.

My friend Lindsay Brady is a hypnotherapist. He is highly respected and very accomplished at removing people's unwanted habits from their lives. His starting point is this: "Our perceptions determine our behavior."

If we perceive ourselves to be nonsmokers, it would never occur to us to smoke. But if we perceive ourselves to be people who smoke, then we will also live into *that* perception. That is what the brain does. It pictures things (right brain) and then figures out a way to live into that picture (left brain). The brain does that all day long.

If we perceive that the dark bush behind the tree that moves in the wind at night is a bear, then our fear is real, as real as if it *were* a bear because perception is as important to the brain as outside reality is. To the brain, perception *is* reality.

If you *perceive* my remarks to be a criticism of you, then that's what they *are* to you, even if I didn't mean them to be. To the brain, perception is everything.

The key to eliminating the hold of a habit is to change our perception. To perceive ourselves as nonsmokers, nondrinkers, or daily walkers is to change our whole life's behavior in the literal wink of an eye. The eye perceives one thing then it winks shut. After the new programming, it opens to a whole new perception, a whole new life.

HOW TO START A NEW HABIT

All we really have to do is send the brain the picture of what it is we want, the behavior that we want. Picture it as already our habit. In the now, not in the future, in the now. Being who I need to be to have this intention fulfilled *now*.

After that it's a matter of practice. Enough pictures create a clear intention. The deeper the intention, the stronger the sense of purpose. Practice takes it down to the soul.

It doesn't matter how long I've had the habit. Behavioral change expert Brady says that a ninety-year-old woman who has been smoking since she was twenty goes through *exactly* the same process in quitting as does a nineteen-year-old woman who has been smoking since she was eighteen.

All that matters is whether I am ready to live a new perception and purpose. Then through slow, repetitious, lazy enjoyment of the new habit, I maintain the new way of being. I confirm the perception by gentle repetition, and after a while the new habit sets in and begins confirming itself without any effort from me. Changing is nothing. Maintaining is everything. From the top of the mind to the bottom of the soul, the new way of being becomes a part of who I am. Tom Peters once wrote about habit replacement in his newspaper column:

One morning, in Houston, almost five years ago, I was a non-exerciser. For a series of not very profound reasons, I went out at 5 A.M. and took my first, bumbling speed walk. Eleven minutes later (OK, quite a few nanoseconds), I was hooked. Every day I fret that I'll renege. It's a lifetime pursuit, which causes pain some days (e.g., as I write, it's unseasonably cold, rainy and getting late). But as of this morning, I was a no-baloney, world-class, rudely dogmatic exerciser.

It *is* that simple. Honest.

Tom Peters is right. It *is* that simple. People change in a nanosecond. People go from smoker to nonsmoker in an instant. People go from drunk to nondrinker in a heartbeat (as long as the heart can still beat). People give up their pills the instant they throw the last handful of them into the toilet, watching them disintegrate in cloudy, wet powder trails just as former habits are disintegrating too.

Whether I've had my habit for two years or twenty years, the process is exactly the same. How long I've been doing something means nothing. The action I take to create a new self-perception means everything.

I remember when I was a beaten man taking the path of daily drunkenness. I couldn't tell you why I was doing it anymore. It was a very common and popular force of habit. Beaten people sleepwalk down the path of life without any thinking or sense of purpose.

And then one day, I received a refreshingly honest letter from a friend, and my perception began to change. After a while I could actually *see* myself being someone who was clean, sober, and happy. I could picture it.

"I can do this," I said to myself. "I can be this." And my perception became my reality. The lie is that "the longer I have a habit, the harder it is to break." The truth is this: "The longer I have a habit, the more fun it is to break."

I am actually a paranoid in reverse. I suspect that people are secretly plotting to make me happy.

—J. D. Salinger

PEOPLE REALLY
UPSET ME

Most people believe that you can't teach a person new tricks. Therefore, when I teach a seminar on "reinventing yourself," people are skeptical about the whole subject of change. You can imagine some of the questions I get.

"I try to be optimistic, but my boss always upsets me. What can I do about that?" asked a woman recently.

"Step one would be to admit that you are lying to yourself about the situation every time it happens," I said in my happiest voice.

"Lying?"

"Yes, lying. You are lying. You just lied to me and the whole room too. And thank you for having the courage to ask this question. You are asking it for everyone else who didn't have the courage to ask it. Are you willing to stay in the conversation with me even though I might have just said something offensive to you?"

"Yes!" she said with a laugh.

"You are lying when you say that your boss upset you because your boss did *not* upset you. Your boss does not have the power to upset you. You can only upset yourself. That's the only way the upset can happen, when you yourself think upsetting thoughts and send those thoughts to your body. Your upset can only come from what *you* think. It can't be caused by what somebody else thinks."

"I don't understand that, because it sure *feels like* he's upsetting me."

"Yes it does. Just like for thousands of years it felt like the world was flat, so people believed the world was flat. But once we started changing our thoughts, and thinking the world was round, it began to *feel like* it was round. When we saw ships' masts come up on the horizon, we processed those sights into our new thinking, and pretty soon everyone *felt like* the world was round. You can do the same thing with your thoughts about people upsetting you. Once you think correctly enough times that you are actually upsetting yourself, then it will also feel that way too. It will no longer feel like people can upset you. Imagine how good that would be."

"How does that relate to my feeling upset when my boss is sarcastic with me?"

"If you would begin to think differently, you would begin to feel differently about it. You would understand that it is something *you think* that is upsetting you."

"I still don't believe that."

"Let me ask you a question. What if you had won the lottery the night before, and you were coming to work to put in your two-week notice because you were going to take your $10 million and move to Hawaii and start the business you always wanted to start. Can you picture that?"

"Yes. I like picturing that."

"Okay. Now what if your boss stopped by your workstation and said something sarcastic to you about your work? How would it affect you on this fine day?"

"I'd probably laugh at him. Or tell him where to go. I might even give him a big hug and thank him for modeling the perfect opposite of the man I want to have in my life. I could do lots of things."

"Would any of them upset you?"

"No, not on this day."

"So do you see that your boss really doesn't have the power to upset you? That you could be thinking about something, like living in Hawaii, that would absolutely eliminate any power he had over you?"

"Yeah, but that's $10 million. Give me $10 million and I won't let *anyone* upset me."

"No, it wasn't the $10 million, it was your thoughts *about* the $10 million."

"I don't see that."

"Okay fine. Good. Stay with me. Now what if, after you laughed at your boss, you double-checked your lottery ticket against the morning newspaper, and you suddenly realized that you were one number off. You really didn't win the lottery after all."

She began to smile.

"I wouldn't like that," she said. "But I think I'm getting this. It wasn't the money because there really wasn't any money. It was the thought. I thought there was money, but it was just a thought. It was the thought that made me happy, not the money."

YOU MADE ME WHAT I AM TODAY

If I feel upset after someone says something, it was what I *thought* that upset me, not what they said. It is always what I think. Most of the time I deliberately "forget" that to feel is actually to *think-feel*. I "forget" this truth because it's easier to make other people responsible for my emotions, especially if those emotions are out of control.

Even when I do admit that my thinking causes all of my feelings, it still seems hard to control. It still seems like a fire hose out of control. I keep chasing it, picking it up, and directing the water at something, but then it twists away.

People who are unwilling to take the time to practice their thinking leave themselves out of control and vulnerable. They are not vulnerable to other people's moods, but vulnerable to their own habitual responses to those moods. We are creatures of habit, most of all, in our reflexive thoughts about other people. A person who can hurt our feelings can hurt us a million more times because we've started a habit about how we think about them. Our thought habits, not other people, determine the emotional lives we live. Outside circumstances are meaningless compared to the way we think about them.

A SUCCESS THAT WAS UNIMAGINABLE

The other day I received a letter from Ronald, a man who had attended a seminar I gave on creating relationships. He wanted me to know what taking the course did for him:

I came away from your seminar with the most profound turning point in my life so far. I realized I had to make a commitment to move back to Montana to be with my daughter if I was ever to have a chance at a close relationship with her. So in July of 1996 I moved to Billings, Montana, where my daughter was living with her mom. I also started a new company at that time.

The success in both my business and my personal life is unimaginable. I make a six-figure income monthly now, and my relationship with my daughter is everything I hoped it would be. I travel the world now with my business to Singapore, Australia, Brazil, Hawaii, the Philippines, Japan, the Caribbean, Spain, and Portugal. I am truly blessed.

But what happened for Ronald was not *caused by* me and my course. It happened *inside of* the course, and more importantly, inside of his mind. In the course, he opened up his mind and created a purpose inside this clearing. He did it himself, and there was no way that I could have done it for him. The most I could do was suggest a line of thinking that might lead him to the source of his own power, to his soul purpose in life. In his case, the suggestion was used and it worked. In some cases it does not.

Why do some people leave that same seminar unmoved? I believe it's because people become afraid when they discover the awesome power they possess to set aside their feelings and get into *action*. The power of the human mind to create the future scares them. It may be fear of the unknown. They have accustomed themselves to having all the power in life originate on the outside, in circumstances and other people. They've learned to live that way, reacting to others all day, all week, all year. It's a way of life that's easy to fall into. You just tell yourself enough times that people upset you, and it will feel like the truth.

WHEN THE SPIRIT GROWS TIRED

"Hell is—other people," concluded French philosopher Jean Paul Sartre, after reacting to others all his life. He had constructed a theory of life that concluded that a human being was a "useless passion" living a meaningless life. But like most philosophers, he was not describing life itself, he was describing *his* life. From the point of view that he chose, he was defeated from the start. Then, because he was brilliant with words, he constructed an entire philosophy called "existentialism" around his own low emotion. People with similar lazy spirits can read Sartre and confirm for themselves that there is something wrong with life itself.

Sartre convinced himself that the only valid human response to the world was "nausea." But nausea is a failure of the will. Nausea is energy failure and the swimming, sickening feeling we get when we are convinced that we can't stomach other people. But it's just an invented feeling.

To say that someone upsets me is a lie I'm telling myself. Because I could, if I wanted to, choose *not* to be upset. The reason I don't want to choose that is because it's easier to feel than to think. Thinking about people, my commitments to them, and my love for them takes courage and imagination. If I am afraid of developing my courage and imagination, the easiest way out is to lie. The lie is that she upsets me. The truth is that I can respond to her any way I want.

One of the finest thinkers of our age has been Marilyn vos Savant, the person who has the highest IQ ever measured.

She wrote a weekly magazine column, and I was always intrigued by the simplicity and power of her intelligence. One time a reader wrote to her about the difference between thinking and feeling:

Dear Marilyn,

What is the difference between thinking and feeling?

Colleen Kelley

Spokane, Washington

Dear Colleen,

Feeling is what you get for thinking the way you do.

Marilyn

For the personality, bankruptcy or failure may be a disaster.
For the soul, it may be grist for its strangely joyful mill, and
a condition it has been secretly engineering for years.

—David Whyte,
The Soul Aroused

WINNING THE
LOTTERY
WOULD SOLVE
EVERYTHING

I have heard it said that the lottery is God's way of pun-
ishing people who are bad at math. But I believe that if God
really wanted to punish people, he wouldn't just have them
keep losing. He would let them win.

The whole concept of the lottery is based on what
Gandhi insisted was one of life's few true evils: unearned
money. It is the concept that ruins more businesses and individuals than any other: something for nothing.

When people begin to tell themselves that money itself
is what's missing in their lives, the lying has begun. Because

money is not what's missing. What's missing is the ability to make it and keep it. Action builds that trust, and we lie to stay out of action.

In his book about lottery winners in the state of Michigan, *Money for Nothing*, Jerry Dennis documents many sad stories of people who won millions, only to have their lives become much more difficult. One couple won a fortune, only to face tax complications that prompted them to quit their jobs and invest in a small resort. The main resort house began falling apart as soon as they moved in, and the whole thing turned into a nightmarish money pit. People started treating them differently. Even the grocer, who used to smile and give them a nice deal on vegetables or throw in an extra orange, never did that any more. People regarded them coldly.

Lottery winners often have to move to another state and start again. They go somewhere where people don't know how they got their money. Because people treat lottery winners much differently than they treat people who have earned their wealth. Distant relatives call and ask for financial help.

"Come on! It's for my daughter's medical bills. It's not as if you earned that money. You ought to be willing to share some of it! I can't believe the selfishness and greed you're showing. After all, it's just by pure chance that you have that money. I could have won as easily as you. It's pure luck. You didn't do anything at all to deserve what you got. And now you won't even share a small percentage of it! I know people who work hard for their money who are more generous than you. . . ."

A wealthy person who has *earned* his or her money is usually treated with respect. I saw a television show on which Bill Gates and Warren Buffet, both multibillionaires, went to the University of Washington to share the stage and speak to students about their business and life experiences. When the two men arrived in the auditorium, they were greeted with a standing ovation.

People who become millionaires in the lottery are often treated with jealousy and a kind of contempt. The universe has a great deal of fun unmasking the lies that we tell, like the lie about money solving everything. Most people who win money quit their jobs and try to spend their way to happiness and fulfillment, only to find themselves growing less and less happy. Many realize that they were not even being truthful with themselves every morning when they said, "I hate this job."

Joe Mullich, writing in *Business First*, recounts the horrible misadventures of lottery winner Buddy Post, who won $16.2 million in the Pennsylvania State Lottery.

When Buddy Post won his $16 million, he was a cook and carnival worker, working for every cent he had and treating his money as if he had earned it, which he had.

After winning the lottery, Post began a life of pure trouble. He started a bar and a used-car lot with his siblings, but those businesses went under. Post's landlord then claimed that Post owed her half the lottery money, and Post was restricted from taking any more of his winnings. Eventually she got a third of it. Around the same time, Post's brother, Jeffrey, was plotting to kill Post and his wife. He was trying to get the rest of the lottery money for himself. The brother was convicted of attempted murder in 1993. Post then declared bankruptcy with debts of $500,000, not counting money owed for taxes and to lawyers. Mullich concludes his story about Buddy Post:

Today? Post lives in a mansion, but the gas was shut off when he couldn't pay the bill. Post now says he feels lucky his phone and electricity weren't shut off too. Post has been trying to auction off his future lottery payments but the Pennsylvania Lottery is trying to block the auction. Post says he will devote the remainder of his days to filing lawsuits against lawyers and others who have conspired to take his money

The reason that unexpected horrors fall upon so many lottery winners is that they have tried to equate their discipline problems with money problems. They tell themselves that money is the answer when it's not. The answer is action. How to develop a reliable course of action that would provide more than enough money. They lie to avoid this action.

In *Money for Nothing*, Jerry Dennis concludes that "Many lottery winners have been disappointed to find that, instead of a free ride on a gravy train, they've only been given a new pair of shoes for the same old dusty road, or, as one winner put it, 'the same problems, just with bigger numbers.'"

In a shocking study done by Dan Coates, Ronnie Janoff-Bulman, and Philip Brickman, the well-being of lottery winners was compared to those who had suffered accidents resulting in quadriplegia (loss of the use of arms and legs) and paraplegia (loss of the use of legs). They wanted to find out whether people who won the lottery would have huge increases in happiness, and whether people who suffered such devastating physical traumas would have huge *decreases* in happiness.

Neither thing happened! The increases didn't occur, and the decreases didn't occur. People kept their happiness quotients, on the average, at the same level no matter whether they lost their legs or won millions of dollars. The two groups reported almost no change in their levels of happiness.

So people could win the lottery, or they could lose their legs. The two events would have the same effect on their happiness in life. I think that proves that happiness is a separate thing. It's totally separate from outside events, good or bad. It's an *internal* adventure, and it's based on our ability to grow a sense of purpose that we can fulfill. To continue to tell myself that I'd be happy if I won the lottery is to continue to lie to myself about where happiness comes from.

There are many ways to victimize people. One way is to convince them that they are victims.

—Karen Huang,
The Humanist

THEY'RE TOO BEAUTIFUL FOR THIS WORLD

This is the Vincent Van Gogh lie. And the Billie Holiday lie. And the Kurt Cobain lie. And the Marilyn Monroe lie. And the Janis Joplin lie. And the Dylan Thomas lie. That there are people who are just too beautiful for this world. The world has let them down.

This "too beautiful" lie is used to let the sensitive artist in all of us off the hook. If we are too sensitive and beautiful for this crass world, then we don't have to come to terms with it. We don't have to interact with this world responsibly or decently. Because we're too beautiful for it. We can act like drugged children, crash our lives, and have this lie excuse us until the end of time.

The lie says that the person is too sensitive. The crude world has repeatedly done the person wrong. That's why he took his life.

But that's not the truth. The truth about Vincent Van Gogh, for example, is that when he painted, he was beautiful, but in other matters he was not.

In the conduct of his everyday life, Vincent Van Gogh was not a man of great beauty. He was always encouraging his emotions to work their dark magic. His arrested emotional development was obvious in his letters to his brother Theo. So it's true that Vincent ought to be admired for who he became when he had a paintbrush in his hand. But to admire his *entire* sorrowful life and make it a part of his legend is to be very confused.

Because many other artists *do* learn to make a success of their private lives, living and evolving gracefully into creative old age, it is ludicrous to *honor* Vincent Van Gogh for his indulgences, weaknesses, and suicide, or say that they were caused by his inner beauty.

When Vincent Van Gogh committed suicide, he shot himself artlessly. There was no beauty in it. He shot himself in the stomach, and it took him two agonizing days to die.

To make that another "beautiful" part of him, and then somehow feel guilty that we didn't provide him with a world that was as beautiful as he was, is just lazy thinking. It is thinking that should be ridiculed.

Contrast his immaturity and self-indulgence with the elegance and wit with which painter Georgia O'Keefe lived her personal life. Even in her seventies, she was happy and physically beautiful. She retained a spirit and energy for life that *matched* her great paintings.

IS THAT ALL THERE IS?

The "too beautiful for this world" lie is perhaps most powerfully illustrated by a near-masterpiece of mystery novels, Martin Amis' *Night Train*. The final premise of the book is that there are people so beautiful and bright that the rest of the world can't measure up to them. Other people, less perfect than they are, disappoint them so!

"I didn't ask to be born," says the too-beautiful person.

And later, even though they didn't ask to be born, they are heard to describe life as a terrific letdown. Is that all there is? When given even the mildest tests for logic, this position doesn't hold up.

Here we have a novelist, Martin Amis, who has risen so high in his craft that he can write such a brilliant book, and yet his final message (wrapped into the solution of his mystery) is that we humans are not worth the effort. In other words, life is a bitch and then you die.

This is what is so illogical about that. Martin Amis, with his glorious and captivating writing, is showing us how high humans can really fly. He is modeling for us how geniuses would write if they wrote mysteries. And then he argues that there is no real human genius, that humanity is a disappointment.

He is caught in his own self-deceit. And as proof that he is not telling the truth, I submit to the jury *his own book*! Martin Amis unwittingly proves his pessimistic philosophy is a lie because anyone who could write as powerfully as he does is *affirming* humanity's possibilities for beauty even while attempting to deny them.

It's as if Nureyev were to walk out on the stage and say "No one can do this!" and then proceed to thrill us with his gravity-defying dance. When we watch the thrilling performance of a Nureyev, we are hit with the truth like a train in the night: Human beings are magnificent.

A SLIGHTLY OFF-BALANCE GENIUS

It isn't just the world of art that has embraced pessimism, which is the laziest and easiest intellectual position to take and defend. The media have also been pessimistic beyond reason.

Magazines like *Time* gave "The Unabomber," Ted Kaczinski, a tremendous amount of coverage and respect for his wild, superstitious manifestos written about the horrors of technological life and the dire consequences for our future.

They printed a huge amount of his insane writings and stroked their chins wisely as they considered whether or not this poor man wasn't just a slightly off-balance genius with an insightful message for our times.

That he had blown people's faces and limbs off with his murderous letter bombs seemed to fade from significance as the media considered the huge intellect that would rage so profusely against technology and the future. The Unabomber's intellectual position, however, was pure psychotic paranoia and superstition: There *shouldn't be* technology. There *shouldn't be* change. Life *shouldn't be* the way it is.

Like a spoiled, frightened, angry child stomping his foot at reality, Kaczinski ranted and raged in his long writings, and the media ate it up and hinted that it might be prophetic and brilliant.

Then came the debate about whether our misunderstood genius should receive capital punishment or not. A man who deliberately and calculatingly murdered, mutilated, and maimed many innocent human beings in the most cowardly way with his letter bombs? Why yes, that's a tough call.

As the debate went on about whether he ought to be executed or given the Nobel Prize, I arrived at what I believed to be a viable compromise. The Nobel Committee should perhaps send him a long, thoughtful, and official letter that acknowledged his breakthrough thinking in the area of technology, and it could be set up so that when he opened the letter, it would explode and blow him to kingdom come.

LEFTOVER LIFE TO KILL

A feeling of joy in being alive is humankind's birthright. That almost every child celebrates this joy daily is something that most writers and artists (former children themselves) either can't or don't want to remember.

Another person too beautiful for this world was Kurt Cobain, lead singer of the grunge-rock group Nirvana. He committed suicide at the height of his popularity. Those around him at the end report that he had lost his will. He let his will grow weaker and weaker from lack of use. He was "bored" with life and strung out on heroin, which is like a chemical version of his own hollow, empty, passive death. He blew his head off with a shotgun. All who knew him viewed his suicide as unwise, given the talent he had and how much life he had left to create with.

When the poet Dylan Thomas did the same thing as Cobain (only Thomas used alcohol as his weapon of choice), his widow, Caitlin, wrote a book about it called *Leftover Life to Kill*. The White Horse Tavern in New York City, where Thomas downed eighteen straight shots of whiskey and keeled over dead of alcohol poisoning, *celebrates* the occasion with pictures of the great poet on its walls. Even today artists and drinkers go there to get in touch with the spirit of someone who was too beautiful to live in this world. I used to get drunk there myself, shaking my head sadly at the photos of the ill-fated poetic genius. I was an idiot.

The Buddha spoke about the one thing Kurt Cobain and Dylan Thomas never seemed to think about cultivating: will. And when the Buddha spoke about Nirvana, he meant the state of mind, not the group:

"Will is the way to Nirvana," said the Buddha. "Laziness is the way of death. The wise man guards his vigor as his highest possession."

Taking the long view, it is easy to see that high-self-esteem people are happier than low-self-esteem people. Self-esteem is the best predictor of happiness we have.

—Nathaniel Branden,
Six Pillars of Self-Esteem

YOU HURT MY
SELF-ESTEEM

I was meeting with a group of Native American leaders in Arizona on the subject of running their gambling casino more efficiently. They were considering hiring me to deliver some seminars on the owner-victim distinction.

All of a sudden, one of the leaders said that the young people in their community had a problem.

"What's the problem?" I asked.

"Our problem is self-esteem," she said. "Our young people, especially, have trouble with their self-esteem."

"That's usually at the bottom of everything," I said.

"And I can give you a reason why," she said.

"What's that?"

"Well, it's things like Donald Trump. Recently, Donald Trump opened a new casino in Atlantic City, and the tax deal that the government gave *him* was better than the deal our casino got. Things like that make a negative impression on our young people and hurt their self-esteem."

"Really? How does that work? How does that hurt their self-esteem?"

"It's pretty obvious. If we're not treated as well by the government as someone else, it's going to affect our self-esteem. Especially with young people."

"I am afraid that I don't quite see how."

The room grew quiet.

"Would you mind if I explained what I mean?" I said. "I mean, if we are going to be doing workshops together, then it's very important that you know exactly how I feel about this matter of self-esteem and your young people."

"Okay, sure!" she said, happy to have a little debate going in a meeting that had threatened to become predictable.

I walked to the whiteboard at the front of the room and wrote the phrase, "self-esteem" on the board. I then drew a very large arrow pointing to the word "self."

"There's a clue," I said, "to where self esteem comes from. There's a clue to the origin of self-esteem right here in the word itself. There's a good reason that it's called *self-esteem* and not some other kind of esteem."

I decided to continue talking.

"Let's picture one of your young people hearing about the deal that Donald Trump got. That news is just a piece of information. It doesn't have the power to raise or lower self-esteem by itself, because it has no meaning. It doesn't mean anything. Nothing means anything until we assign it meaning. It's just a piece of information. Can you see that? It's what the young person *does* with that information that affects his or her self-esteem. Your self-esteem comes from something you do in response to an external event. It does not come from the event itself. It's always an inside game."

"What if there's nothing they can do?" the leader asked.

"*Whatever* they do, including nothing, will have an impact on their self-esteem," I said.

"How do you mean?"

"Self-esteem is a result of our own opinion of our own actions. There is *no limit* to the actions we can take. Even if the actions initially fail to get an immediate result, self-esteem can increase, *just from taking the action!* Self-esteem is always related to action, to what we *do,* not to what people think of what we do."

"I still think the tax break to Trump was unfair."

"Of course it was unfair! And you all face unfairness every day. It's what you *do* about it that matters. Actions are the only things that can gather the inner strength called self-esteem. That government bureaucrat who made the decision to give Donald Trump's casino a more favorable deal *doesn't have the power* to hurt the self-esteem of your people. It's how your young people *respond* to what people do that matters. What if your people were to object to the unfair treatment? What if they were to get some people together to visit their congressman? What if they also visited the local newspaper and talked to the editor? Let's work with response techniques. Let's get good at it. Let's have some fun. Let's make some bureaucrats wish they had never messed with us."

"We have special circumstances. It's harder for us."

"I agree. But raising your self-esteem is up to you. You can build self-esteem in a prison cell, in solitary confinement even. It does not depend on the thoughts or actions of other human beings."

"Our young people need more praise."

"That can help if we're praising *actions* they have taken. But when we praise our children for nothing, that doesn't automatically raise their self-esteem. Getting them to wear 'I am unique' buttons is an insult to their intelligence. A mud taco is unique. Praising their *actions* is what helps because it encourages the child to *do more* of what he or she just did to win the praise. But it is in the *doing* that their self-esteem goes up. When my child comes in excited at having learned to ride her bicycle, my congratulations are just icing on the cake. Her self-esteem is already sky-high from what she *did*. Did. Doing. Doing. Doing! Praise by itself does not raise self-esteem. Action alone raises self-esteem. No one else can raise my self-esteem, although someone can certainly help inspire me to action."

LISTEN TO THE RADIO

I heard a sports talk show host say on the radio that Dallas Cowboys superstar Deion Sanders was "raising the self-esteem" of Cowboys' fans with his flashy football heroics. I grabbed my phone and called into the show to remind the host that Deion Sanders can't do that.

He can certainly entertain the fans. He can even make some of them forget, for a brief shining moment, their own low self-esteem. But it's a brief moment. In the long run, he can never raise *their* self-esteem with his performance, he can only raise his own.

"Yeah? Well, whatever," said the talk show host.

When I finally owned up to the fact that no one could raise my own self-esteem but me, I obtained a certain freedom to act on my own behalf. This took me longer than it takes most people. But there is no age limit to it. I've seen people in their sixties begin their lives fresh and new with a whole new sense of self-confidence and self-respect.

I took over the controls of how I felt about myself pretty late in life. I returned self-esteem to its original source: my own mind's evaluation of the action I was taking.

Prior to that time, I was fibbing about where it really came from. I was saying that other people were raising and lowering my self-esteem. I was pretending that statement was true because pretending excused me from taking action. I would finally convince myself that I didn't have enough self-esteem to do the things successful people were doing. The lie was serving its purpose: no action.

Now that I've dropped the lie, I can raise my self-esteem any time that I want to. I do it the way everyone else does it—by acting more boldly, more completely. And I can lower my self-esteem too, if I don't watch out and stay honest. I can lower it by quitting on myself.

No other person has anything to do with either of those options.

The American family travels to strange places in order to take photographs and bring them back, as if the photographs will serve in future years as data-points, crystals of memory to give emotional resonance to experience that was originally without any.

—Norman Mailer,
Of a Fire on the Moon

IT'S A SHAME
WE DIDN'T
CAPTURE THAT
ON VIDEO

I think death gains power over us when we begin to worship our own past. When we do everything for nostalgia and have no fresh new future. We transfer all power to the past. It is important to notice that the past can waste our lives when we use the past in this way. It makes the present feel empty of its promise.

There are some people who think that almost everything that doesn't honor the past is a shame. Therefore, almost everything that happens is a shame. And everything that didn't happen is even more of a shame. Life consists of moving from one kind of shame to another.

The shame game is a result of attaching exaggerated importance to the past, of pretending that the past has an emotional resonance that the present doesn't have. Lying about the superior power of the past has a purpose: it keeps us from enjoying the present and inventing the future.

This creates a life governed by a molding stockpile of memories. This old stockpile is combustible, it catches fire, and it burns down any chance we have of being great right now. All shame comes from memories. And constant, repeated feelings of shame come from allowing memories to dominate our lives.

"It's a shame we didn't capture that on video," my family members tell me.

"Why?" I ask.

"So we can watch it later!"

"Why would we want to do that?"

"For the fun of it. So we can look back and remember old times."

"Oh all right," I say, giving in.

But they can see that I'm gloomy about watching family videos. Secretly I'm thinking to myself: What fun will this really be? Won't it just reawaken the "good old days" lie? Why not get together and enjoy being alive *now*? My family notices my gloom.

"You're never any fun," they say to me. "With your psychological ideas. Videos will be final, bittersweet moments of remembered fun when our days have dwindled down. When we groan out loud every time we get up out of an easy chair. In other words, when we are old, we will want to watch videos of when we were young."

◆   ◆   ◆

I remember when I took my son, Bobby, to kindergarten for his first day at real school. I was startled at how many parents were there with video cameras to capture the event of their children's first day. It was something like a yuppie nightmare. The whole event became an event *about* the cameras. The teachers shy and annoyed in front of the cameras. The kids not knowing what to do. Some parents, without cameras, ducking under the cameras to say good-bye to their children. Apologizing to the cameras.

What I noticed most on that day was the fear on the faces of the little children whose parents were holding and operating cameras. They were scared just being at school the first day, and rather than having a parent there to hold them, look them in the eyes, and tell them that it was going to be all right, they instead saw their parents with black electronic appendages coming from their faces, barking shrill orders ("Look up Jason, look up, look up here!" "Jennifer! Jennifer! Jennifer, honey, don't do that, put your hand down, look at your teacher Jennifer! Look at your new teacher!"). In the confused eyes of the children, the whole videotaping fiasco added to the feeling of being abandoned. In future years, watching that videotape of Jennifer's first day at school, family members will comment on how frightened Jennifer looked, and it will make them uncomfortable to watch it ("Oh, look sweetie, you were so scared! I didn't know you were so scared to go to school. Oh, I can't watch this, can we skip this and put on the delivery-room video of when Megan was born?").

◆　　◆　　◆

I was on an airplane not long ago, trapped in my seat next to two people who were talking very openly to each other. The man and the woman had just met, but they talked to each other loudly for the whole flight, and it was a nightmare flight for me because of it. All they talked about was their past and what a "shame" this was and how "sad" that was. After a sad story the man told about business betrayal, the woman said, "That's a shame, that's sad." After the woman's story of how her ex-husband treated her, the man said, "That's sad."

It went back and forth over and over, and I was silently going crazy. They talked on and on about the past, and they ended each story with both of them saying, "That's sad." I must have heard them say, "That's sad" about three hundred times during the flight. I finally found myself wishing the plane would crash. I wished the captain would come on and tell us to put our heads down between our legs because he was going to have to land on this upcoming mountain.

"Now *that's* sad!" I would say to those two storytellers. "You want sad? This is sad! This is a real shame," I would say, pointing out the window at the flaming wing.

I am tired of dramatizing the past or of being obsessed with memories of the past. So to me, it's not really a shame that I didn't capture the past on video. It's a shame when I do not capture the present. That's the only true shame. When I neglect to invent a *current life* worthy of seeing through the video lens of my mind.

We lie about the superiority of the good old days to keep ourselves out of action. We focus obsessively on the past to keep us from exploring the unknown and uncertain beauty of what is right there in front of us.

Thinking that the self must remain constant for life to have meaning is like falling helplessly in love with an inch.

—Alan Watts

THAT'S JUST THE WAY I AM

I claim all kinds of permanent characteristics. They get me out of things. They let me off the hook. They are lies, but I have taught myself to believe them.

I say, "That's the way I am."

I am asked whether I have introduced myself to the new person at work, and I say no. I am shy. That's just the way I am.

I am asked whether I remembered my aunt's birthday, and I say no. I am forgetful and disorganized. That's just the way I am.

My child asks whether I remembered a promise made and broken, and I say no, but yes, now that you bring it up. I am so sorry. I am so hassled and busy. You know how stressed I get. I get stressed out. That's just the way I am.

Why didn't I speak up in our team meeting at work? Why didn't I object to that new system that I know will not work? Well, you know. You know me. I don't like confrontation. I say live and let live. Give them enough rope and maybe they will hang themselves. I don't have to get into it with them. I always keep a low profile. That's me. That's just the way I am.

However, whenever I wake up from this self-deceit, which is more often every day, I get excited. I give talks. I write books. People can feel the excitement.

I remember meeting an airline pilot in a health club that I was visiting early one morning in Phoenix. He was on the treadmill next to mine, and we began a conversation that revealed that we shared many of the same interests. I told him that I would send him a copy of one of my books. After I mailed it to him, I didn't give it another thought.

Then one day this letter arrived:

Just a quick note to thank you for sending me your book. I am the American Airlines pilot you met in the health club in Phoenix. Well, as sometimes happens, the very day *100 Ways to Motivate Yourself* arrived, my wife, Shannon, and I brought into our home a lady we met recently who had fallen on hard times. We learned that Linda was in the state-run mental hospital here in Houston because of an attempted suicide. She had recently lost her job due to a problem with depression. Her medical insurance was canceled, she was broke, living alone, and well, her life stunk.

Linda came home with us that evening and we soon moved her belongings into our garage. She was very depressed and was spending a lot of time in her room. So I had the idea to bring her up the copy of your book. She reluctantly began reading, and we began to see signs of her recovery almost immediately. The book has been at her nightstand for almost forty-five days now and she refers to it each day to give her the direction she needs.

Linda's rebuilding of herself was slow. And sometimes there were painful setbacks. But when those inevitabilities would occur, she would refer to the book and soon she was *pumped!* And back on track.

I am very happy to report that Linda now has a career position with a major corporation here in Houston. She is goal-oriented and is much, much happier. We credit much of her success to your book.

Linda could have spent the rest of her life saying, "I get depressed. I am depressed a lot. That's just the way I am."

But it obviously didn't take much to change the way Linda saw the world. In fact, at any time, at any moment, we can change the way we perceive things. We can change our fundamental way of being. It doesn't take much to get this process going. Sometimes just a little book on a nightstand will do it.

All Linda had to do was allow for the *possibility* that she could teach herself to be a self-motivated person. She made a seemingly small decision to open her universe. (The human brain has been referred to as the three-pound universe.) She decided to let the light of reason begin to guide her, instead of the self-pitying emotion that had been guiding her before. As Colin Wilson says, "Reason has its miracles too."

There wasn't anything in that book that Linda didn't already "know" on some level as a deeper truth, a perception that resonated and harmonized with her soul. While her brain felt like it was learning it for the first time, her soul had already known it to be true and simply confirmed it for the brain by sending up that "yes!" feeling. The soul is always saying "yes!" when we release a lifelong lie.

Enough of those "yes!" feelings and you get the huge peak experience that Aikido founder Morihei Ueshiba received when he finished a long and exhilarating martial arts workout session and cried out, "I am the universe!" That experience is never completely forgotten once it is experienced. Since the word "universe" seems literally to mean "one song," the "I am the universe" experience can become the one great song that you can't get out of your head.

GETTING HEAVY WITH THE LIE

Selling myself on "the way I am" keeps me locked in my own fearful childhood. I become heavy with a false claim of permanent personality, heavy with the lie. That's why becoming enlightened and growing up feel like the same thing.

En*light*enment can really mean making yourself lighter. Many people actually lose weight when they become enlightened. As each lie is let go, they rise up, feeling lighter and enlightened by the process.

To throw aside the heavy lies that we are struggling to carry around with us is to become free, which is everything. It's growing *up*. It's growing lighter, higher, freer.

Immanual Kant said that enlightenment is a person's emergence from "self-imposed immaturity." Self-imposed immaturity is when we *deliberately* lie to ourselves and become frightened children in the face of adult challenges, instead of becoming brave men and women who are simply challenged by the tasks ahead. We do this because it feels easier and more familiar to us. In truth it is far more difficult and is actually abnormal. If only we knew.

Joseph Sobran began one of his newspaper columns recently this way:

Arthur Koestler told the story of an old priest he met during World War II. Fascinated that the man had listened to thousands of confessions and heard countless intimate secrets, he asked him what he had learned about human nature.

The priest was naturally reluctant to discuss the secrets of the confessional, even in the most abstract terms. Finally, though, he offered one generalization: "Basically, nobody ever grows up."

MAKE OF OUR HANDS ONE HAND

If you leave a long night of poker playing and someone asks you the next day, "Did you win last night? Did you win any money?" It would probably never occur to you to say, "No, I was dealt a bad hand." Because, of course, you were dealt many hands, over and over again.

And because cards follow the laws of statistics and probability, the bad hands and the good hands eventually even out. It's always *what you do with the cards you have* that determines the outcome, not the cards themselves.

And that is true for life as well. It would be a lie to say that life dealt you a "bad hand," because even as you are saying those words, life has already dealt you another hand. Each breath may be said to deliver another hand. Life deals you hand after hand.

Most people sit on the first hand they were ever dealt and say, "This is just the way I am." This is a form of liar's poker that is played by people who do not understand the real fun inside the game of truth.

Take the "hand" of singing, for example. Most people believe that they can't sing, That they weren't born with a very good singing voice. Some people were dealt better voices than they were.

"No thanks, I'm no Frank Sinatra," the man says, chuckling as he is asked to go along to a carol-singing party. "I can't sing. That's just the way I am!"

But let's stop for a moment and think about Frank Sinatra, who most people believe was dealt the lucky hand of a naturally wonderful voice. He was always a good singer. That's just the way he was.

In the 1940s, when Sinatra was trying to catch on as a singer, there were many male vocalists who were popular crooners in the age of the big band. Sinatra did not have any spectacular vocal advantage over any of them until he made a commitment to create one.

He wanted an edge, something that would set him apart from all the other performers of the day. He wanted to become extraordinary. So he decided to go swimming. And he swam and he swam. He wanted the kind of strong singing voice that could sing a long musical phrase without gulping for breath, so he swam laps underwater.

"I began swimming in public pools," said Sinatra, "taking laps underwater and thinking song lyrics to myself as I swam holding my breath."

After six months of dedicated swimming, Sinatra began to feel his lungpower dramatically deepening. There was no more shallow chest breathing. Now he could breathe deeply into his abdominal cavity and hold a note for a heartbreakingly long time. Finally, he had created the edge he was looking for.

"Instead of singing only two bars or four bars at a time," Sinatra said, "like most of the other guys around, I was able to sing six bars, and in some songs eight bars, without taking a visible or audible breath. That gave the melody a flowing, unbroken quality, and that's what made me sound different."

Oh, so *that's* what made Frank Sinatra sound different! And I always thought it was a natural gift he was born with. A genetic blessing. A genetic full house. The kind of hand I never got dealt myself.

When I say, "That's just the way I am," I am asking for complicity in my lie. I am asking you to nod your head and accept that I have permanent characteristics that dictate what I do. I want you to agree that who I am is beyond my control. I have no control. I have no power. I am helpless and hardwired.

It's funny how our society conspires with us to keep the "that's just the way I am" lie alive. Until finally, when it's so obvious that someone has truly changed, we can't deny it any longer so we jump to a secondary lie: something (or someone) changed them!

We should face the truth: People reinvent *themselves*. They do it all the time. But look at how we deny it.

If someone who used to be drunk all the time is now living in sobriety, we immediately attribute that to something *outside* of them. "Look what the Betty Ford Clinic did for Martin!"

Almost all personal change is attributed to outside forces. "Look what Jennie Craig did for her!" "The church saved his life!" "JoAnne turned Paul's life around for him."

Our greatest problems as humans come from confusing the outside with the inside. People change themselves internally all the time. Day and night. And the method of change is *always* an internal intention to change. To swim. To work hard. To really go for it. The reinventing person can then use external support, but it is not the source of the change. The source of the change runs deeper than that.

Give my regards to oblivion.

—Dr Zachary Smith (Gary
Oldman) in *Lost in Space*

WHAT DOESN'T KILL ME MAKES ME STRONGER

Many rock, rap, hip-hop, and pop stars have celebrated the idea of drugging the soul. They have even urged the practice on their wisdom-seeking young fans. Tote that bail, lift that barge, hit that bong.

When rock groups began using psychedelic drugs they wrote songs in which they advised us to turn off our minds, get high, and merge with the universe. The songs *claimed* that this, after all, is not the same as dying. But is it really not dying?

Ask Janis Joplin. Ask Jimi Hendrix. Ask Elvis Presley, Kurt Cobain, Jim Morrison, Keith Moon, and Brian Jones. And it's not just rock stars. Ask F. Scott Fitzgerald. Ask Dylan Thomas and Ernest Hemingway. Are the pages of this book numerous enough to list all the names?

One remembers John Lennon's descent from experimenting with LSD and heroin. Lennon and Harry Nilsson appeared in nightclubs, drunk and high with sanitary napkins tied to their heads. Eyes glazed like those you see on corpses, they were practicing death, wearing dress rehearsal rags.

You hear a lot about the banality of evil, but it is nothing compared to the banality of alcoholism and drug addiction. Once people wrap that trap around them, they are no longer worth studying because the addiction itself explains their decline. As people, they become grotesquely boring.

We try to explain their addiction by saying it was "the pressure of fame," and we attribute it to all kinds of psychological factors, such as grief or insecurity, but it is never any of that, it is just addiction. Boring, brutal, banal addiction.

I remember in my youth buying into the idea that great writers drank because they had to. Their wild, creative minds needed something to soothe the fire of insight that separated them from other people. I'd fall under the spell of Norman Mailer's writings on the manly power of alcohol to illuminate and give offbeat color to a world run by dull bureaucrats. I bought into William Faulkner's claim that "a writer without whiskey is like a chicken without a goddamn head." I agreed with Dylan Thomas' glorification of the drunken poet, inebriated with the beauty of the word.

I thought it was ultracool that the Grateful Dead could get so strung out (ask Jerry Garcia) that they could fill a whole concert with two songs, jammed endlessly in a time warp of looped memory loss. Turn off your mind and float downstream. This is not dying.

When I myself finally became addicted, I told myself that I was probably just like Norman Mailer or Ernest Hemingway. Now I'm really a writer! Tortured at the soul, misunderstood, I needed a layer of drugs and alcohol to cover such an exposed and sensitive nervous system. We poets need that. Those of us who are poets know what we're talking about.

THE SUN ALSO SETS

It never occurred to me to face the real truth of what life was like for drunks and addicts like Hemingway. Because when looked at in the sober light of a soft spring morning, the glamor of Hemingway's drinking life seems to not be so glamorous after all. It's not so much fun to read about either.

But later as I became clear, I learned to read again. I learned that Hemingway's alcoholism caused him to experience kidney and liver trouble, edema of the ankles, cramps, chronic insomnia, blood clotting, high-blood uremia, and skin problems. He also became impotent. He was prematurely aged. And as Paul Johnson chronicles in his insightful book *Intellectuals:*

> Hemingway's father committed suicide because of his fear of mortal illness. Hemingway feared that his illnesses were not mortal: On 2 July 1961, after various unsuccessful treatments for depression and paranoia, he got hold of his best English double-barreled shotgun, put two canisters in it and blew away his entire cranial vault.

This is not dying?

I was a speaker in a poetry-writing contest while a senior in the creative writing program at the University of Arizona. I showed up so drunk for the evening that I have almost no recollection of it. My poor mother was in the audience, and when she woke me the next morning from my blacked-out condition, I asked her in pure panic whether I had *showed up* for my reading.

"Oh yes," she said wearily. "You were the life of the party."

The pathetic, self-pitying, autobiographical poem I read that night was rather ironically titled "I Only Shame Myself," which is a line from the Marlon Brando film *One Eyed Jacks*.

A KNIGHT OF THE LIVING DEAD

One day not long after that reading, I received a letter from my friend, author Art Hill, himself an alcoholic who had been clean and sober for a few years. His letter took me by surprise:

> You say that you drink for pleasure, to increase the adventure in your life, but I can tell by how you write about your drinking that this is not true. . . . I don't know whether you will ever want to speak to me again after I tell you what I'm about to tell you, but I'm willing to risk that because of how much I care about you. You don't drink because you're a writer, or because you are misunderstood, or because you enjoy it, or for any of those reasons. You drink for one reason: you are an alcoholic. You are an alcoholic no

different and no better than any other alcoholic. You are exactly like the drunk in the park with the paper bag around his wine. You drink for the same uncomplicated reason that he drinks: you are addicted. The things you tell yourself about your drinking are lies. You drink for one reason only. You are a drunk.

This is not usually the kind of letter that builds one's self-esteem. But for me, it was a letter that changed my life. After reading it, I sat there stunned. It was still in my hand as I walked around the house thinking, "What if this is true?"

And although I knew that it *was* true, I had never let the truth in before, not until his letter. And because I admired Art Hill so much as a writer (my final term paper and oral report in poetry-writing class were about his poems), I respected his opinion. And because he himself was a recovered alcoholic, I respected his knowledge of the subject. He said that I had the power to acknowledge my addiction and choose a happy and sober life. I had nowhere to turn but to the truth, which was that I was capable of changing myself.

And the truth did set me free.

If you intend to consolidate and quicken your energy—as I'm sure you do—you will find accepting the truth and living in it to be two of the most powerful concepts one can embrace.

—Stuart Wilde,
The Quickening

I AM
HELPLESS

There are lies that make news, lies that public figures and celebrities tell. There are also simple everyday lies, lies that everyday people tell to avoid embarrassment. And then there are lies to the soul.

A lie to the soul runs deeper than any other kind of lie. It is like a river designed to chill something deep down inside of us. It's a lie whose unconscious mission is to kill the spirit, remove the passion, and deny our uniquely human power.

The lie is created to convince us that we have no power. That we are helpless. But it is not true that we have no power. The truth is that we have so much power, it sometimes scares us.

As Nelson Mandela said, "Our worst fear is not that we are inadequate. Our deepest fear is that we are powerful beyond measure."

Because of that fear, we lie. We are powerful, but we lie and say that we are not. I too am a liar. I am not as much of a liar as I used to be. I don't lie as often, not as bad, not as deep. But still, I am a liar. I lie to make myself feel helpless. I lie to stay out of action.

I lie about the power of circumstances. I say that circumstances prevent me. I say that circumstances and other people are more powerful than I am. I claim that they are always favored over me. Then I turn the lying inward. I say that I am defective. I am so defective that I am helpless. I am more helpless than Neil Young at his most helpless, when he sings, "Helpless, helpless, helpless."

On a dark and lazy level it seems to work for me. If I seem helpless *enough,* maybe someone will *help me.* Someone powerful. Someone with money. Someone with love. I then become ashamed of how helpless I am.

That's when my friend Steve Hardison looks me in the eye and says, "You are in the habit of making yourself feel ashamed because it keeps you out of action. Shame keeps people out of action. You shame yourself in order to remain passive."

I am ashamed to admit that he is right. And in the end, the "helpless" lie works. It chills the body. It works! The body curls up. The body goes to sleep. The mind follows suit.

Because I am human, the main racket I run in my life is convincing myself and others that I am a victim. Circumstances hold me back. People don't appreciate me. They don't thank me enough. They don't pay me enough. They don't understand me.

In this practice, I am not alone. In this practice, I am joined by everybody else. All of us do this. Some of us do it all the time. Some of us do it some of the time.

The way out for me was to finally allow myself to listen in on my own conversations. I became a total eavesdropper on my own talks to myself. I became more and more aware of what I was doing to myself. This felt good. Because awareness was the way out. It was the way out of the deception. Because awareness provided an opening for action.

The goal of self-honesty is awareness. Awareness first of the lies, and then awareness of the truth. I can say that there are seventeen lies we tell in life, but underneath, there is just one lie. All lies to the soul are the same lie.

The lie is that we are helpless.

The truth is that we are powerful.

FINDING YOUR
DEEPEST POWER

The chief reward of surrendering innocence, so that the soul may be fully expressed, is an increase of power. In the presence of deep power, life becomes robust and passionate, signs that the soul is engaged, and being given expression.

—Thomas Moore,
Care of the Soul

THE TRUTH IS THAT WE ARE POWERFUL

I remember a time in Tucson, Arizona, when terror gripped the town. I was living there with my family in a nice neighborhood on the east side of town, and nice neighborhoods were the target of the terror. There was a psychotic serial rapist at large known as the Prime Time Rapist. His habit was to terrorize entire families during the evening hours when families had finished dinner and were usually all together watching something on prime-time television.

He would tie families up, rape the women, assault the men, and create fear and havoc everywhere he went. For months he would invade homes and strike whole families, never coming close to being caught. Some families were so traumatized by his invasions that they left town forever.

One acquaintance of mine, who lived not far from my house, hired armed guards to watch his home around the clock. The entire community lived in fear.

I remember visiting my father's home during this period of time. He said to me, "If he ever did that to me and my family, I wouldn't want to live. I wouldn't want to live after that."

I won't even talk about what this man did to the families he assaulted, because it's too horrible to ask you to picture it. As his attacks increased, he became even more vicious. Soon he began hitting homes at all hours of the night, abandoning his earlier prime-time modus operandi.

I was feeling great anxiety whenever I read about the rapist. I had a family with three beautiful young girls in it, which exactly fit the profile of the kind of victims he was in the habit of raping and torturing.

SOMETHING IN THE AIR

One night, as I lay in my bed not quite asleep at around two o'clock in the morning, I felt a funny feeling in my stomach.

I sat up in bed, and the odd feeling increased. I can't describe the coldness I felt, but the closest I can come to describing it is to say that I felt as if I was in the presence of evil.

Keep in mind that at that time, I was the least superstitious person you would ever want to know. I didn't believe in telepathy or any other kind of weird paranormal powers. I was a total skeptic about things like that.

But that night the feeling was real, and I couldn't ignore it. I slowly got out of my bed and picked up the baseball bat that I kept in the bedroom. I've always believed that a baseball bat was the perfect weapon for home self-defense because no one would ever get close to you if you were swinging one, and if they wanted to shoot you from a distance, there wouldn't be much you could do about that anyway.

Holding my bat low, as if I wouldn't mind using it on someone, I started slowly walking through the house. We had one of those typical Arizona homes that was spread out over many rooms on one level. I walked through them all, still feeling the presence of something awful near the home. As I walked through the rooms, I remember seeing the moonlight shining in the big picture windows. I remember looking in on each of my three sleeping daughters, thinking of how innocent and beautiful they were, sleeping in the pale blue light of the moon. If evil was near, I wanted it to see me.

So I walked slowly from room to room, slowly rotating my bat in my hands, ready to hit something. I walked for what seemed like an hour.

Then, as quickly as it had came, the feeling disappeared. All of a sudden, I felt completely light and free. The cold shivers left me, and I felt warm all over. The bat seemed ridiculous in my hands, and I decided to go back to bed. What was I, some paranoid ex-ballplayer hoping to get a chance to be macho? I went back to sleep.

The next morning, I woke up and got ready for work. I remembered the incident in the night, and I wondered about it because what I remembered most clearly was *how real the feeling of evil was.* The other thing that surprised me was that I was also very clear that the right word was *evil.* It was not "something dangerous" or "something weird," it was more than that.

I drove off to work but didn't go far from my home before I saw two ambulances and a long line of police cars outside a house just a block away from ours. As I slowed down, a female officer waved me through. I rolled down the window and asked her what the matter was.

"It was him," she said. "He struck last night."

Tucson had been so thoroughly terrorized by this man that she didn't have to explain who she was talking about. She knew I would know.

"What time did it happen?" I asked.

"A little after two o'clock," she said. I nodded, feeling the strangest lack of surprise I have ever felt. Some part of me already knew. He was right there, outside my house.

Whatever signals I had picked up that night were very real. And ever since that time, I have been much more open-minded about the huge potential we humans have to tune in to the universe when we need to.

Most people think that human beings are weak and vulnerable. In some ways we are, so if you want to keep that lie alive, you can. But in most ways we are not. We are very powerful beings, powerful beyond our wildest imaginings. The more we look into the depth of our powers, the more we see. Eventually they caught the Prime Time Rapist. He committed suicide while surrounded by police officers at his house.

That morning in Tucson, I became a believer. We are much more powerful than we let ourselves know. We only use a tiny percentage of our power during the average day. But once a crisis appears, a purpose appears, and we find it all. We take ownership of our lives.

THE IDEA OF
OWNING
YOUR LIFE

I spent three years on the road teaching seminars based on my book *Reinventing Yourself*. The purpose of the seminars was to show that "reinventing" begins with seeing that you are not really a victim. It ends in learning to be an owner of your own life.

On the road, people have been very excited to be reminded that deep down they *are* owners of their own lives. It is possible for them to be the boss of themselves, just as when they were small children, able to be boss by saying, "You are not the boss of me!"

Somehow putting it in the words *owner* and *victim* has fired people's imaginations. Remember that fierce possessive feeling you got when you yelled out, "mine!" as a small child? That's the ownership that I saw people connect to in the courses.

Try this experiment: Go up to a tiny child, one who can just barely speak, and touch something that they are clinging to, just rest your hand on it gently, and whisper to the child, "Mine." Watch what happens. Watch the child snatch it away wildly and yell, "No! Mine!"

We love ownership. We love possessing. We love holding something close.

People also see that when their energy is low, they can become addicted to being victims. They can waste their most precious moments pretending that they are being victimized. People see that and laugh. In my courses, they laugh and laugh. Some people tell me afterward that they have never laughed so hard in their lives. They are laughing at themselves, at the distorted positions that they have taken as victims. Distorted. A psychological game of Twister.

The fact that we always have a choice makes for an exciting workshop. Because people can really see the choice, and they get busy strengthening their capacity to choose.

They're building up that trigger finger on choosing owner-ship so that they can pull the trigger more easily. Soon they are able to just squeeeeze the shot off: I own it! Mine!

When that shot is taken, all power flows back into the owner. Boom! The situation no longer has the power. The spouse no longer has the power. The company no longer has the power. The *Dilbert* cartoons can be pulled down from the wall. The walls themselves can come tumbling down because they no longer have the power. We have it in our hands to own our lives.

It's funny how people didn't remember inventing them-selves as children. But even when they were little, and their parents said that they *were* someone, they knew that wasn't true. They weren't anyone until they made up someone they wanted to be.

When an adult can do that trick—make up someone they want to be—they become powerful beyond measure; the power to invent a person is so wonderful that it's almost addictive. Look at the lines in front of the movie theaters. Robert DeNiro isn't able to make enough movies; did you notice? Once he got rolling, he worked day in, day out, week-ends, nights, four o'clock in the morning. Why? The ultimate human invention—creating characters. It's the biggest thrill in the human experience.

"Although I'm not usually a huge fan of abridged audio-tapes," a woman from Pennsylvania wrote me in a letter, "I must tell you how much I am enjoying *Reinventing Yourself.* It is information that I desperately needed to hear, and more important, apply in my life. I have been trapped in a victim's role since my husband's tragic death two years ago. The wisdom projected in your sense of humor is helping me to realize that I don't have to stay in that role . . . that I am still very much alive. Thank you."

Humor shows us that we are still very much alive. Humor is the key to seeing our own comic self-victimization. A laugh opens us. Without a laugh, we seriously defend the victim lies we are telling. We deepen our position in self-pity. We get swallowed up in it.

Have you ever been swallowed by a boa constrictor? It's one of the most *annoying* experiences you could ever go through. We tempt that huge snake whenever we start telling ourselves that we are victims.

The truth is that we don't have to do that. The truth is that we all own the deep power of self-control.

WHO CONTROLS YOUR SELF?

It has been said that only the disciplined are free. And intuitively, maybe we know what that means. But do we know it consciously? Do we know it in a way that we can *use* every day?

Actually, we human beings have just begun to learn the power of self-control. It's a field that has almost no information in it yet. It is a new frontier of human exploration and adventure. So far, we can only hint at its true potential.

For hundreds of years, self-control was thought to be something that only a few people had. It depended on our having a certain gene, perhaps, or something permanent in us: a *characteristic*.

But we are now learning that it depends on no such thing. The truth is that self-control is simply a skill. Like the skill of playing a guitar. It is something any and all of us can learn. As we continue learning, we can learn more chords. We can learn more songs. We can learn more of everything. We can be the Eric Clapton of self-control. Because self-control rocks.

Self-control is fun because it is the one form of control that is not frightening. Other forms of control happen from outside. They come rudely crashing into our lives and frighten us. Some kind of control will happen, no matter what. You will always have some kind of control influencing your life. The only question is from where. Will it be control from the outside (frightening) or control from the inside (exciting)? If we don't develop *self-control*, we will be controlled by *others*. It is going to be one or the other.

When we are immature, it is as if we prefer our control to have some kind of outside element. Some person outside ourselves who will make us happy. Or some fortunate external event. Some so-called "good thing" happening.

That was true for me for far too many years. My happiness was way out there. It wasn't anywhere near where I was. I used to dream that it would somehow come to me. Some happy situation. Some opportunity to be totally free. My ship! I just knew it would come in. Little did I (let myself) know that it was harbored inside of me all along.

I was being very hypocritical not so long ago. I was teaching one way of life and living another. Looking back on it, I can see that I was a milder version of one of those disgraced television evangelists caught cruising for prostitutes in the church's Cadillac.

In my workshops, I was teaching the difference between taking ownership of your life and being a victim. I was teaching that self-victimization leads to a life of passivity and regret. I was teaching how to lead a proactive life of ownership.

Yet I myself was being a victim all the while, complaining bitterly about being overloaded with endless seminars and workshops that took me away from my friends and family, had me on airplanes, and in hotels for most of my "difficult" life. I was temporarily a self-made victim of my own success. It was all a lie.

TOO MUCH ACTION, SO I LIED

I was not being straight with myself. I was lying so that I wouldn't have to take responsibility for my own schedule and my own life. That looked like it involved too much action, so I lied.

During that time in my life I recall watching a television special about Karen Carpenter. She died of anorexia at the end of some long concert tours. I remember watching it and saying, "She was not a victim. The Carpenters didn't have to tour that much! They had many million-selling records. They could have stayed home or done moderate touring. They *chose* their schedule. They had free will! We all have free will."

Yet the television show continued to make the Carpenters out to be victims of the greedy record company. They were forced to spend each night in a different city. No sleep. Amphetamines. No food. Victims.

I shook my head. I rolled my eyes. I felt smug and all-knowing. I couldn't see that I had put *myself* in the same situation. I wasn't being honest with myself about who was running my life. *I* was running my life but pretending that others were.

Then one day in an airport, weary from a long seminar and waiting for the plane that would take me to my next city, I happened upon a passage from Kierkegaard that I had written in my notebook:

"The principle of limitation is the only saving principle in the world. The more you limit yourself, the more fertile you become in imagination."

I quickly tracked down one of my favorite books by the optimistic British philosopher Colin Wilson, and I began to reread it. I was excited all over again. I was able to see clearly that Wilson was right when he said that Kierkegaard's principle of limitation is the recognition that *human happiness depends on self-discipline.*

It's funny how when you are on to something, the whole world starts to affirm it for you. Soon after I'd read the Colin Wilson passage, I happened to see a television news story about prisoners of war. I was flipping through the channels, and I stopped. It was based on a study of men who were war prisoners for two or more years in Vietnam. The study showed that later in life, the former prisoners were healthier, physically fitter, and happier with their lives than other men their age were. In other words, the imprisonment seemed to have had some kind of *beneficial effect* on their lives. The severe limitation of imprisonment made them more active and alive when they got out.

I thought of my father and of my friend and mentor Steve Hardison. Both had harsh memories of being in financially challenged, fatherless families when they grew up. And when they became young men, they earned money with a vengeance. Both became millionaires at a very young age. The power of limitation!

Not long ago, I had lunch with two men in their late thirties who had emigrated in their teens from Iran to the United States. They told wild stories about how destitute and deprived their lives had been in Iran, and about how excited they were to come to the United States. They began their professional careers by opening a small body shop for car repairs in San Antonio, Texas. Today they own over fifteen of the finest new car dealerships in Texas, and they recently turned down an offer of over $3 billion to sell their business.

"You people don't know how good you have it in America," one of them told me over lunch as he laughed over and over again at his own stories of how he and his friend fought through prejudice and misfortune to finally succeed in the car business.

"Most Americans don't understand that they live in paradise. They live in the middle of such unlimited opportunity, and they don't even see it. I wish everyone here could live for a few years in Iran. Boy. That would be even better than giving them one of your seminars. A year in Iran! Would they ever be different when they returned to the States! They would succeed like crazy!"

We can see clearly how *limitation* can inspire huge compensatory efforts. How it can lead to astonishing inventiveness. It has helped me understand what the philosopher Fichte meant when he said, "Being free is nothing, becoming free is heaven."

ONLY THE PARANOID SURVIVE?

That also explains what Andrew Grove meant when he said, "Only the paranoid survive."

Grove, who headed the wildly successful Intel Corporation, wanted to always guard against complacency, the sense that we have already arrived, that we are already free.

By conjuring up an invented sense of paranoia, Grove kept his company *alert* and *alive*. He asked his people to imagine competitors everywhere and to attack their own company's vulnerabilities in the marketplace. He then asked his people to get "scared" enough to do something about it. To outsmart the competition even when the competition was just imaginary. It was like kids playing soldiers.

"Look out!" one kid will shout to another.

"What is it?"

"Look over there, behind those trees, the enemy! They're attacking us from behind!"

"Come on, let's move out! We can head them off if we can get over that hill before they see us!"

And kids will go racing across the hill in the vacant lot, just in time to head off a would-be enemy surprise attack. It is fun. It is exciting. It is the pure joy of "Let's pretend they're after us!" That's the exact spirit of inventive play and innovation that Grove has shrewdly tapped.

GETTING MAD AT SELF-CONTROL

Sometimes an old word or phrase can take on an emotional history, and you can end up *hating* a phrase like self-control. "Self-control" can become a trigger for resentment.

When I was growing up, it seemed to me that I heard the word "self-control" *only when I lacked it*. It became a phrase with a negative emotional history. Anything that is used repeatedly to shame us is going to lose its true usefulness. It will lose its power to become a tool that helps us build a powerful life.

Yet self-control *is* a tool that gets us a powerful life the more it is embraced and developed. It's as if all of life were a piano concert, and self-control was our practice on the piano.

In my imperfectly recollected childhood, I am hearing the term "self-control" used against me. It is used even more in my adolescent years. It's something that is recommended to me sarcastically. It is something I obviously have none of. Soon the very sound of it makes me mad. This is why growing up is harder than it needs to be: the emotional resonance of words.

Soon I was defying the very thought of self-control: "What? Self-control! I don't *want* any of that. I don't want to be a puritanical, conservative, neo-Nazi, robotic clone of you. Sorry."

When Peter Pan defiantly sang, "I won't grow up! I don't want to be a man!" it struck a chord with many of us who felt the same way. I've since looked back at that story and thought that it might have derived its enduring popularity from its glorious defiance of all that was difficult in life.

But is growing up really so difficult? Is it so hard to become organized? To consolidate the spirit? The truth is that the minor discipline (and self-control) involved with growing up actually makes life less difficult and more adventurous, less stressful and more enjoyable. If only we had known.

But because I didn't know, it was nearly impossible to embrace self-control as my salvation when I was so resentful of it as an idea.

A KIND OF PERSONAL ANARCHY

Some of us were so angry about being accused in our youth of not having self-control that we were drawn to its opposite, which was a kind of personal anarchy that we might have called "self-expression."

We wanted to be free to drink, eat, and grab pleasure any time that we felt like it. That was our rebellion against the shame of having no self-control. Hey! We'll make self-control *wrong!*

We were sloppy and called it "natural." We were disorganized and called it "spontaneous." We were undisciplined and called it "creative." We were fat and called it "having a beautiful spirit inside." We said that the inner person would shine through, right through the fat. See that dull glow coming through the fat? One beautiful person shining on. We all shined on, like the moon and the stars and the sun.

This was the dawning of an age. We were always high on something, and we called it *rising above* a lame old world.

We became huge and short of breath. We were getting out of shape. Misshapen! We all began to look like David Crosby. And all of this because we were mad at self-control.

But soon that anger began to fade. We began to see something. We began to see the connection between self-control and happiness. We began to realize that only the disciplined were free.

IS IT PLEASURE OR HAPPINESS?

Self-control can begin with being aware of the difference between acting toward my own happiness and taking pleasure. Pleasure is a temporary sensation, and happiness is enduring. Pleasure disappoints, happiness does not. Knowing the difference is a huge step.

For example. Perhaps I take great pleasure in the sensation of chocolate cake being in my mouth and being swallowed. Mmmmmmm! That's real pleasure!

But once the cake is swallowed, my true happiness remains unaffected. In fact, my happiness might even be negatively affected, if I eat too much and feel sick and get fat. The cake can lower my self-esteem. I've never heard this exchange in all my years of human conversation:

"You look happy. Why are you so happy?"

"Who me? Oh, I'll tell you why I'm happy. Three hours ago, I ate a large amount of chocolate cake!"

And that is how pleasure and happiness have come to be at war with one another. They seem to the immature person to be the same thing, which is why immature people become pleasure seekers. It appears to be the same thing. A very famous, nationally known, compulsive womanizer was described by one of his lovers as being "just like a little boy." Another said, "He's such a child. He brought the mother out in me." Gag me.

Pleasure shopping is the same. There is a kind of immature and infantile pleasure taken in buying something that is unnecessary. My thirtieth pair of shoes. Our real power in life comes, instead, from resisting the temptation, from embracing limitation, from saying we have enough shoes for now.

That's where all the power in life comes from. It comes from the sense of control cultivated *inside* of us. Not from waiting for some good fortune to come floating in randomly from somewhere outside of our control. That "good fortune" is always an illusion. There's no real truth to it.

FINDING YOUR SOUL PURPOSE

It was just a few years ago that I happened upon the most remarkable person I have ever met. He was a business consultant who had just been hired by a corporate training company I was working for. His name is Steve Hardison, and you may have heard of him by now. He's been written about in many newspapers because of his success as a consultant and personal coach. I have also written about him in two previous books.

When Steve first started coaching me, it was a wild and bewildering experience. It was like having Vince Lombardi, Joan of Arc, and Anthony Robbins all in the same body, coming at you with an energy and compassion that often left you stunned.

After one of our earliest sessions together, I believed that I had really found my true life. I walked out of the meeting with him feeling like I could see everything differently. Even the leaves on the trees seemed cleaner, clearer, and richer in color. I was in charge of my life!

But soon it began to collapse around me. Small problems with the children came up. They began to fight, and everyone in our household started to work their emotional magic until the usual chaos reigned supreme. I was getting confused and disoriented. Small things went wrong. The garbage bag I was carrying outside split open. The oil light in the car went on. A storm came unexpectedly out of the desert sky, and a huge tree fell in the backyard. A phone call from a bill collector cut into the dark mood that was surrounding me. I wondered, "How could I have felt so good and in charge just a day and a half earlier and so lost right now?"

So I went to the phone and called Steve. I didn't feel great about calling him at home, and I could tell that he was busy with his family, but I explained my depressed state of mind and asked him to recommend something.

"Stay in touch with what you're up to," he said.

"With what?" I asked.

"With what you're up to."

"My overall purpose?"

"What are you up to? Figure out what that is."

Then I remembered. Our meeting earlier in the week was about being "up to something" in life. It was about living on purpose and playing full-out. I remembered that I was "up to" being a contribution, an ongoing contribution to the people I loved, to myself, and to my clients.

The minute I thought about this, my whole sense of being in charge of my life returned. The split garbage bag looked comical. The tree looked "cool" to me and the kids as it lay collapsed across the yard in the rain. Life was dramatic and real. I felt alive again.

NO PROBLEMS LIKE MONEY PROBLEMS

In a recent meeting with Steve, I told him that I had traced a lot of my money problems earlier in my adult life to my relationship with my father.

I told him how my father was raised, poor and penniless, working from an early age to help his mother save money.

His own father abandoned the family, and his mother (my grandmother) and her children had to work around the clock to make the money.

My father succeeded with a vengeance. He went to night school after returning from World War II. He rose quickly in corporate America, and he knew the value of a hard-earned dollar.

But I did not. In fact, my father was so rigorous about good, hard work that I knew from the start that I would never measure up. I would mow the lawn, and it would never be right. I was the opposite of him as a boy. Because of his huge success, we lived well in a suburb of Detroit. I was a dreamer. I spent my time reading and inventing. I was not good at work because I hated to work. When my father came home to look at the job I had done mowing the backyard lawn, he would come inside shaking his head, disgusted.

"You don't deserve your allowance," he would say.

I hung my head. I knew that there was something missing in me that he had. Some gene for hard labor. Then he would go to his room and emerge in shorts and a tee shirt.

"Come on," he would say. "Let me show you how easy this is."

And I would watch him mow the lawn for me. He would mow in neat rows up and down, up and down, going faster and faster. The sweat would pour off of him as I stood by, embarrassed. I didn't know how to look. So I nodded my head whenever he glanced up at me through the sweat. When he was almost completely finished, he turned the lawn mower over to me.

"Go on!" he said.

I took the lawn mower handles in my hands, and I started to push it to mow the part of the lawn that he had left for me. But something was wrong. Somehow it felt like the lawn mower had just acquired about fifty pounds of extra weight. And something was wrong with the grass. The grass felt like it had just turned to tough plastic. Even though I had just watched him fly through this grass like a man possessed, which he was, somehow I was struggling, barely moving the mower in fits and starts.

I watched him look at me. He was disappointed. He raised his hand, made a circular motion, and shouted something that I didn't hear.

"What?" I said, glad to stop.

"Keep going, keep going! Get *after* it," he said.

And he turned to walk into the house. I don't want to get after it, I thought. I don't care about this lawn. I *like* it when it grows tall and free. Why does he have to have our back-yard look like a buzz cut on an army guy's head? Maybe because he was in the army. Soon I began imagining my father in the army, a war hero flying planes, shooting down the enemy. I wondered if I could ever do that. Probably not. I'd probably go *over* to the enemy. If I were captured, I'd offer them anything and everything they wanted from me. I was not like my father. I was the opposite of my father. I was more like my mother, God help me, afraid of absolutely everything.

As I continued thinking these thoughts, I heard the screen door slam. My father stood there glaring at me, this time with a can of Blatz beer in his hand.

"Do you think it will get done by itself?" he asked.

"No," I said, with my head hanging down.

"What were you doing?"

"Nothing."

"You were doing something, what was it?"

"I don't know."

"Well, let's see if I can help you. Were you mowing the lawn like I asked you to do?"

"No."

"Why not? Why weren't you?"

"I was thinking about . . ."

"You were thinking?"

"I mean, I don't know."

"Were you thinking that maybe I wouldn't come back out, and you could get away with not finishing the lawn?"

"No."

"Do you want to earn your allowance?"

"Yes."

"Because right now, you don't deserve any money. Do you think you deserve any money?"

"No."

"Good. Because I work hard for my money. Do you realize that? Do you know when I wake up earlier than you do and go to bed later than you do that I have been working?"

"Yes I do. Thank you."

"I don't want you to thank me. I want you to learn to do some work yourself. I've never seen you do any real work. Do you know that? You've never done any real hard work have you?"

"I don't know."

"You don't *know?*"

"Well, I mean, I think I have. But I don't know if you would think it was work."

He looked at me for a long time, then shook his head and went inside. These kinds of conversations happened quite often as I was growing up. Whenever my report card came home, they happened. Whenever I had been asked to do some difficult chore, and I only partially did it, they happened. When I received my badges in Cub Scouts, he questioned whether or not I earned them.

"How did you get that patch?" he would ask when he saw it on my blue uniform.

"I did the tasks you have to do. They're in the book," I would say.

"Your mother signed them? She verified that you did them?"

"Um, yes."

"She signed them whether you did them or not, didn't she?"

"No!"

"I know you and your mother."

And he was right. There were some tasks that I did, but there were some that mom and I agreed were too hard for a boy my age to do. So she just signed them because my intentions were good.

"You tried," she would say. "That's all that matters. You tried."

"Thanks for signing it," I said, happy that she understood. I was not like my father. I could not plough through tasks like a mad robot. I was sensitive about how hard things were.

HE SEEMED SO GLAD TO HAVE ME

My father's disapproval would not have affected me so much if I had not idolized him the way I did. And if I had not loved him the way I did. He wasn't angry with me all the time. It was really only when it came to work and money. In all other things, he was warm and compassionate, and he seemed very glad to have me as his son.

There were so many great things about my father and how he raised me that it became incredible to me, sitting in my meeting with Steve Hardison, that whenever I thought of him, I only thought about the things that I resented. How hard I had to work to build up my self-esteem from ground zero in the area of work and money. From the age of twenty-five on I almost always outworked everyone I ever worked with. I was convinced that the words, "you don't deserve your allowance," had become a deep part of my psyche and were responsible for all kinds of problems that I developed later in life. I was convinced that my inability to save money started there. That I believed deep down that I didn't deserve to have any money.

That someone would come take it away from me if they found out that I had any. So I better spend it now and somehow get some value from it before somebody finds out that I have it.

"It's a *lie* that you don't deserve to have any money," Steve Hardison said in a coaching session that I had with him a few years back. "You work even harder than your father worked. Do you realize that? You make a greater contribution to society than your father made. And you have been a single parent raising your children all the while. It's a *lie* that you don't deserve money."

"So what do I do about it?" I asked.

"Stop lying to yourself!" he said.

"But it's in there," I said, pointing to my heart. "It's deep inside me. That I don't deserve it."

"It's a lie."

"But . . ."

"Look, you can stop lying to yourself any time you want. Your past is your past. You have a choice. You can live out your past. Act it out. Reenact it everywhere you go. Or you can create your future. It's up to you. But I think it's time you started creating the life *you* want."

Steve was right. And I had done a remarkable job of changing my entire life around with the help of his coaching. But on a bright day in Arizona not long ago, we were meeting in lawn chairs in front of his home, and I was still talking about the negative effect that my father had had on my habits with money. I had overcome the lie that I didn't deserve to earn it, but I still hung on to the idea that I didn't deserve to *keep* any of it because I was having a hard time saving, no matter how much I earned. I always found an immediate need for it.

"Stop making your father wrong," Steve said.

"What do you mean?" I asked.

"Forgive him. Forgive him completely, so that whenever you think about your father, you are whole and complete. So you can draw strength from what you loved about him. What you loved about him is in you. All his good qualities. They are a part of *you* right now. But if you continue to resent him, you can't use it. You can't draw on it. You'll always feel separate from it. Forgive him. He was only trying to love you. If he grew up poor, he feared you would too. He was afraid for you. Fear shows up as anger and sarcasm in men. So he was afraid. He loved you. He wanted you to be strong and responsible when it came to money. He wanted you to be safe. He loved you."

I had begun to cry because I knew that it was true. I knew everything that Steve was saying was true, and now I couldn't stop crying.

"How long has your father been dead?" Steve said.

"Two years," I said.

"And where is he buried?"

"In Tucson."

"Have you been to his grave?"

"Once."

He let that sink in. He let me realize that the resentment I felt was poisoning the love that I could be feeling from my father. I wanted to talk, but I was choked up.

"On his grave," I said, "it says, 'Man of Steel, Heart of Gold' He never saw me until I was two or three years old. He came home from the war and there I was. I know he loved me. I remember later, when I was a teenager, he used to wake me up in the mornings by singing to me. He couldn't play the guitar, but he would pick mine up and stand over my bed and make up songs to sing to me."

I went on and on about everything I loved about my father. How he became a millionaire industrialist in Detroit. How he fought the unions. How he was approached by the Mafia, stood up to them, and turned them down. How brave he was.

"Forgive him," said Steve.

Every time I paused to wipe some tears away, Steve would say softly, "Forgive him."

RESENTMENTS RUIN OUR LIVES

When that session ended, I felt light as a feather, as if a whole ton of resentment had been lifted from me. My father would live in me differently now. I couldn't wait to tell my own boy, Bobby (named after my father), all the things about my father that I loved and admired. My resentment had run so deep that I had never done that. I had resented my father's alcoholism later in his life, and I had resented his earlier judgments of me, and that was enough resentment to poison my whole memory system. Resentment ruins the life of the resenter. It does nothing to the resented. Why is that so hard for a resenter to see?

I will tell you why it might be hard for a resenter like me to see that. The resenter is not living a purpose-centered life. The resenter is living a memory-centered life.

When I am nursing a resentment, there is no way in that moment that I can be *up to* something.

◆　　◆　　◆

In my next meeting with Steve Hardison, he had an assignment for me:

"You used to be a songwriter, right?" he asked.

"Yes," I said.

"Well, I'd like you to try something. You don't have to do this if you don't want to, but I'd like you to try it."

"What is it?"

"I'd like you to write a song for your father. Just to complete things. Just so that you feel complete with him and can let him be a part of you from now on. What do you think?"

"Okay, I'll do it."

"Bring it here and play it for me next week."

"I will do it." And so I spent a week with my guitar, writing a song for my father. It was not hard to write because I had already become so clear and complete about how much I loved him. But it *was* hard to sing, to get through it without crying.

The next week I sang it for Steve:

SONG FOR MY FATHER

You flew the big planes in the war
And won ribbons for being bold
I didn't even see you

Till I was two years old

But you came home a soldier

With a new little boy to hold

And you've held me ever since

Man of steel, heart of gold

All-star athlete, millionaire

You were a hero that was real

You sang to me in the morning

Heart of gold, man of steel

And you came home a soldier

With a new little boy to hold

And you've held me ever since

Man of steel,

Heart of gold

And I'd give everything I own right now

Just to tell you how I feel

Just for one more hour with my father

Heart of gold, man of steel

And you came home a soldier

With a new little boy to hold

And you've held me ever since

Man of steel

Heart of gold.

RIDING ON THE SOUL TRAIN

Once you are living on purpose, your resentments will simply be obstacles in the way. You will want to clear them off the track as soon as your train slows down enough so that you can feel the power, the deep power of your life's purpose on course.

Listen to what you love. Respond to what you love. Pay attention. Live consciously. Be aware of your own happy moments.

When have you felt most alive? This is how you will find your soul purpose in life. When do you get lit up? What gives you that tingle in your spine? When do you smile in spite of yourself? If you become a purpose detective you will begin collecting clues.

"Nothing inspires me right now," said my friend Fred Knipe during one of those long, lonely nights in college when he and I were up talking about the meaning of the universe. "*You* get obsessed about things," he said. "I don't get obsessed about things."

And I didn't answer him. Because there was something not quite right about what he was saying, although I couldn't put my finger on it. Then a few days later, thinking about what he said, I remembered a few months earlier when

Woody Allen's movie *What's New, Pussycat?* came out. Fred was *obsessed* with the humor in that movie, especially the character played by Peter Sellers, Dr. Fassbender, a frantic, insane German psychiatrist. Fred loved that. He laughed and laughed at that as we went back to the movie many times. For a few weeks he *became* Fassbender. Everywhere he went, he would have people laughing so hard that they cried. I would marvel at him. He's better than Peter Sellers, I would tell myself. How could that be? How could my friend in college be better than Peter Sellers? I didn't trust it, but it was true.

He and I went to the other Peter Sellers movies. We would watch Sellers' masterpiece: Inspector Clousseau. I would laugh, and next to me in the theater, Fred would *really* laugh. I'd look over and see his body doubled over. Those laughs, each one, were communications from the soul.

And now, about thirty years later, Fred has found his true purpose in the character of Dr. M. F. Ludiker, a comedic character he plays to audiences across the United States. It has allowed him to write comedy and to perform, his two loves. It has allowed him to light up people's lives with their own laughter.

Sometimes we come close to our purpose. The truth and beauty of our purpose! And the closer the better. Before he created his comedy, Fred went into songwriting because he listened to how great he felt writing and singing. He once sang on the *Today* show, where he met Barbara Walters! His songs were wonderful. He was living somewhat on purpose, but not inside his true life, not yet. That was not until he became the world's funniest human being.

THE UNIVERSE IS LEAVING US CLUES

As my daughter Stephanie was getting ready for her first year in college, she worried because she didn't know exactly what she wanted to study.

"Study everything!" I said.

"That's how you're going to *find out* what you love. Pay attention," I told her. "Think back to all your times of happiness in life. In grade school, in junior high, and in high school. What did you love the most? What made you happy? Whatever that was, it was a *signal* to you. It was the universe knocking at your door, trying to tell you what your soul's purpose is. It tells you at least once a week. Listen. Listen. Take courses on a whim. Take courses you think are wild and frivolous. Take anything that strikes your fancy. Use your time in college to chase these clues down. Pay attention to your own happiness, and remember at all times that you deserve to be happy. It is your *right* to pursue happiness. Don't get confused by wondering what other people might think. Don't wonder what would make me proud of you. Because I'll tell you what would make me proud of you: happiness. Your being happy would make me the proudest. I don't care if it's music, or medicine, or whatever you want. I don't care if you drop out of college. I don't care at all. I want you to get busy as if you were solving a huge crime. Do you know how the detectives work around the clock to solve the crime? How they put the victims' photos up in their offices just to look at them and help motivate them to find the killers? I'll tell you who the killers are. The killers are the people whose expectations you are trying to live up to. They will kill your spirit. Forget them. They only have expectations for you if they have no lives of their own. If they have lives that they are living on purpose, they don't care at all what you do. They just want you to be happy like they are. It is only the person without a life that criticizes another's life. It is only a parent without a life that criticizes his child's life. Live your own life. Listen to your loves in life. Be a detective of love. Sit quietly in a room by yourself and write down all the things that make you happy. Look at what they are telling you. Listen to the clues. The next time you feel real joy, stop and think. Pay attention. Because that joy is a communication from the universe to you. That joy is the universe's way of knocking on your mind's door. Hello in there. Is anyone home? Can I leave a message? Yes? Good! Well, the message is that you are happy, and that means that you are in touch with your purpose. The point of life is not to *just* be happy, because that can lead to unrewarding pleasure-seeking. The point is to create meaning for your life by living *on purpose*. Doing that, living with a sense of purpose, will give you repeated and recurring happiness. You will feel *good*. And the last thing I have to remind you of is this: it is not selfish. It is not selfish to find your purpose. It is the opposite of selfish. Mother Theresa, Gandhi, Ella Fitzgerald, and Picasso lived in joy. And they lived in joy because they brought joy to others with what they *created* in their lives. What do you want to create? Ask yourself that question every day until it comes to you. What do you want to create?"

The universe leaves us clues. It's just that we don't know, at first, what the clues mean. It tells us what we might do. If we are willing to consider ourselves to be really important people, we can pick up on those signs early in life. Because the truth is that we *are* really important people whose joy *really matters.* Any other statement about ourselves is a lie.

HOW TO STOP THE DECEPTION

How do we stop all this lying? How do we live in truth and enjoy the beauty of being alive? The answer is simpler than it looks. You don't need a brain transplant or a new injection of character or a change of DNA. You might not even need five years of therapy.

A clue to the answer is found inside the purpose of the lies. As we observe these lies, we can see that they are all (each one of them!) designed to keep us out of action. They are all "call in sick" cards on the great game board of life. They make it easy to fall victim to our feelings (especially the negative ones).

The lies give us cover for following those feelings (even though following a negative feeling usually leads to an even more negative one).

Therefore, if each of these lies leads to passivity, then the truth must be found in activity. It is as simple as the saying your grandmother used to repeat to you whenever you helped her with a chore, "Busy hands are happy hands."

Our bodies and minds were designed for movement. They were not designed for an agonized, depressing paralysis. Yet our current culture and society urges us further and further into the soft, lewd arms of comfort. Dark and clammy passivity beckons, and the world becomes obese with self-nurturing. Listen long enough to the lies and we won't move at all. We will just become shimmering mounds of glistening gel, wobbling discreetly in reaction to the latest electronic thrill, the shift of the cushions on the couch, or the blast of the super-sized drink we slurp to wash down another sweet and spicy artificial food. We will shimmer. And we will grow sad. And we will tell ourselves more lies.

Your own way out of this cycle will show up for you once you base your life on constructive action. *What needs to be done?* That's the question. Not, *How do I feel about doing this?* Every time you ask yourself, "How do I feel about doing this?" or "Am I comfortable doing this?" or "Do I have the self-confidence to do this?" or, "How do I remove my fear of doing this?" you are robbing your soul of its greatest gift—the human spirit. You are placing emotion above motion, a near-fatal misjudgment. Emotion is meant to be carried low, and motion high. Lift yourself up, please! The human spirit is expressed in uplifting motion. A bird has to *move* before it can fly. And so must we. Take these broken wings and learn again.

The late and great American philosopher William James said, "Effort is the measure of a man." And Japanese psychologist Shoma Morita said, "Effort is good fortune."

Today there were many people who did not go out running. Why? Because they didn't feel like it. But even the most devout daily runners, the ones you saw out running this morning on your way to work, *didn't feel like it.* Not until they started running. Then, about fifteen minutes into the run, they felt like it.

In our society we have everything backwards. We are all sitting around passively waiting until we *feel like* doing what we know needs to be done. We have now elevated feelings to the highest possible level. We've put them above everything else, and in so doing, we have paralyzed our lives. We have frozen perfectly good lives that could have been constructive and full of joyful accomplishments.

If we would learn to honor movement over passivity, we would have the answer.

The truth is, we *are* powerful. But we can only know the truth of our power by using it. We can't just know it conceptually, because that does us no good. We can't really know anything by just sitting there trying to figure out what we feel like doing.

We knew we were powerful when we were children because we spent the day running, skipping, jumping, painting, laughing, singing, and soaring through space. Our young minds moved, too: creating, inventing, improvising, and making stuff up all day long. As adults, we have talked ourselves into a conspiracy of frozen living. The lies we tell justify the deep freeze we are in, the paralyzed existence. The lies justify and explain why we are always so *stuck*.

Busy hands. That's the answer, and always has been the answer. You'll find your truth, not by believing, but by *experiencing* that your grandmother was right. Busy hands are happy hands.

And if tonight my soul

may find her peace in sleep,

and sink in good oblivion,

and in the morning wake

like a new-opened flower

then I have been dipped again in God,

and new-created.

—D. H. Lawrence,
Shadows

ABOUT THE AUTHOR

Steve Chandler is an author, public speaker, and corporate trainer who appears at more than one hundred seminars a year. He is the author of the bestseller *100 Ways to Motivate Yourself*, a work that received the King Features Syndicate award for 1997's Audio Book of the Year. He is also the author of *Reinventing Yourself* and the audiobook *35 Ways to Create Great Relationships*. He was raised in Michigan and currently resides in Phoenix, Arizona. He can be reached at 100Ways@Compuserve.com.